MANAGEMENT DECISION MAKING

Management Decision Making

A FORMAL / INTUITIVE APPROACH

Jerome D. Braverman

A DIVISION OF AMERICAN MANAGEMENT ASSOCIATIONS

Library of Congress Cataloging in Publication Data

Braverman, Jerome D.
    Management decision making.

    Includes index.
    1. Decision-making. 2. Management—Decision
making. I. Title.
HD30.23.B7   658.4'03   80-65870
ISBN 0-8144-5623-5

First Printing

To Jody

Preface

For the past 30 years and more, applied mathematicians, psychologists, and behavioral scientists have conducted a great deal of research on decision making. Their studies have generally been directed toward the problem of decision making in large organizations—specifically, business, industrial, government, and military organizations. A considerable amount of information has emerged from these studies not only to indicate how people make decisions but also to develop a theory of how people should make decisions. Since some of the decisions required in large, multilevel organizations are quite complex, the theory of decision making, as it applies to such organizations, also tends to be quite complex. However, many such organizational decisions required of managers and executives are amenable to simplification by various techniques that are easily learned and applied. And even the most complex decision problems can be solved if they are approached in a logical and consistent manner.

Consequently, it is feasible to make use of the simpler portions of decision theory and apply them to organizational decision problems in order to improve the decision-making capabilities of managers as well as to improve the performance of the organization. This has been my intention in writing this book. The procedures discussed here have a firm theoretical foundation. Nevertheless, they are essentially very simple. I have attempted to explain and illustrate these procedures in a way that will require of the reader no background other than the ability to follow directions, to reason logically, and to perform some simple arithmetic.

The approach and procedures for decision making described here are not untested. They have been useful in providing solutions to a wide variety of decision problems in all types and sizes of organizations. I am also convinced that most successful decision makers follow these procedures intuitively in arriving at their decisions, often unaware of the precise steps they have taken in forming their conclusions. However, for the majority of executives and managers, whose approach to decision making is at best haphazard, an understanding and mastery of this material should result in a significant improvement in their decision-making performance.

Jerome D. Braverman

Contents

Appendix

MANAGEMENT DECISION MAKING

1

DECISION MAKING AND
MANAGEMENT

Management and decision making are inseparable concepts. We know that all managers must make decisions. We also know that most management decisions must be made under conditions of uncertainty. Consequently, managers must be able to deal with uncertainty if they are to function effectively.

Although uncertainty is prevalent in all phases of human activity, most of us are ill equipped to handle it. The consequences of making poor nonmanagerial decisions are generally not serious enough to warrant the development of a theory of personal decision making, although this certainly would be feasible. However, poor managerial decision making can have serious consequences for the manager as well as for the organization he serves.

THE DECISION-MAKING FUNCTION

Decision making is probably the most important function a manager must perform. No doubt, some managers will argue with this statement, maintaining that some other function such as planning or controlling is more important than decision making.

1

However, on reflection, these managers should realize that every other managerial function requires decision making. You cannot be a manager without making decisions. You cannot be an effective manager unless you can make good decisions.

There are, of course, many different schools of management thought. Some management theorists define management as a process of getting things done through people. Others define management in terms of the functions a manager must perform, such as planning, staffing, directing, controlling, and organizing. However, those who subscribe to this functional school of management do not agree on what these functions are or should be, or even on how many of these functions managers must perform before they are considered managers.

According to the laws of aerodynamics, the common garden variety of bee is incapable of flying. However, the bee, which knows nothing at all about aerodynamics, goes ahead and flies anyway. Most practicing managers know little and frequently care less about the various theories of management. Nevertheless, they somehow manage to manage. Those who manage successfully know, without studying management theory, that decision making is what distinguishes them from nonmanagers. For those who manage poorly, any discussion of management theory would be irrelevant. This is true whether we are talking about the manager of a supermarket, a brokerage office, a manufacturing plant, or an international conglomerate. The primary function of the manager is to make decisions and to assume responsibility for the consequences of those decisions.

Managers make decisions about vendors and prices. They make decisions about what merchandise to stock and how much to order. They decide whom to hire, whom to fire, and whom to promote. They decide when and how much to borrow and what interest rate to pay. They make decisions about expansions and contractions, credit policies, dividends, and plant locations. Managers are decision makers. It doesn't matter whether they supervise ten people or ten thousand—if they make decisions and take responsibility for the results, they are managers. Otherwise they are not.

We hear a lot of talk these days about the "bottom line." The criterion for evaluating a manager's performance is that bottom line. And the bottom line is dollars and cents. A consistently good bottom line means good management. A consistently poor bottom line is usually attributed to ineffective management. However, the bottom line is the result of many decisions made by management over a period of time. Some of these decisions may have been good and some not so good. No manager always makes the right decision. But the greater the preponderance of good decisions over bad ones, the better the bottom line is going to be. It follows that managers can improve their performance by improving their decision-making ability.

How good is the typical manager at decision making? This is a difficult question to answer, since managers and their organizations are not eager to publicize instances of poor decision making. Several years ago a doctoral student in management studied several large corporations and evaluated corporate decision making according to a set of preselected criteria. Approximately 53% of the decisions made during the course of the study were rated good under these criteria. This record is only slightly better than what could have been achieved by coin tossing. And the study covered only successful corporations. It did not include decision making in businesses that went bankrupt, merged, or otherwise ceased to exist.

What might an ambitious junior or middle manager conclude from this rather dismal record of management decision making? If advancement and success in management are at least partially due to good decision making, and if successful managers appear to be right a little better than half the time, then any superior skill in decision making should provide an ambitious manager with a substantial edge in the competition for advancement. More than this, consistently good decisions benefit the organization and in the final analysis show up on the bottom line.

There are, of course, managers whose record of good decisions is far greater than 50 percent. We might ask how these good decision makers make decisions. One thing we can be fairly certain about is that they do not toss coins. Nor do they have advanced degrees in mathematics that enable them to use some set of complicated formulas. We also know that all successful managers do not come from the same business school; indeed, some have never gone to business school at all. Most good decision makers act on intuition. Somehow they know what the right decision is without necessarily being able to articulate the steps they took to arrive at their conclusions. These successful intuitive decision makers do, however, have certain characteristics in common. First, they are intelligent. Successful and even not so successful managers must be intelligent, otherwise they would never have become managers in the first place.

Second, they are thoroughly familiar with all aspects of their field. Management does not operate in a vacuum. Managerial decisions are made with respect to a particular area of operation. All managers must be thoroughly familiar with their own area. The supermarket manager must know all phases of the supermarket business. The brokerage manager, the production manager, the financial manager, and the corporate executive must all be thoroughly knowledgeable about every facet of the field to which their decisions apply.

Third, successful managers are prodigious seekers and gatherers of information. They have facts at their fingertips. And, somehow, they are able to integrate these facts and figures into a coherent picture of the decision situation and arrive at a decision that is more often right than wrong. They do this, for the most part, without mathematical formulas and without computers. They call the process intuition. We call it informal intuitive decision making.

Intuition isn't magic. Nor is it simply good guessing. Good informal intuitive decision makers, either consciously or unconsciously, follow certain principles of information processing that lead to correct conclusions and therefore good decisions. Consciously or unconsciously, they utilize the information available to them in a logical manner so as to avoid erroneous or incorrect conclusions. They also, consciously or unconsciously, assign values and priorities to consequences in a manner that is consistent with the requirements of their job and the goals of the organization.

What the good decision maker may do unconsciously, any decision maker can learn to do consciously. All managers can learn to sharpen their intuition. More to the point, they can learn to use their intelligence and knowledge and the information at their disposal in a systematic manner to arrive at sound conclusions and to make the best possible decisions. All this can be done without resorting to complex mathematical formulas or procedures.

A good decision maker doesn't have to be right all the time. However, he should be right much more than half the time. What might reasonably be considered a good score in managerial decision making? If the typical manager is right only about half the time, he makes one bad decision for every good one. Suppose the manager could achieve a record of two good decisions for every bad one. This would seem to provide a substantial advantage over the average manager. A score of 2 out of 3, or 67%, might then be a minimum goal for any managerial decision maker. Three good decisions for each bad one, or a score of 75%, should put the ambitious manager well ahead of the competition. Such a result is not impossible and can reasonably be achieved with the techniques described in the following chapters.

UNCERTAINTY AND DECISION MAKING

The biggest problem in managerial decision making is uncertainty. Decisions are evaluated on the basis of their results or consequences. But the consequences of a decision can seldom be immediately determined. Consequences and their many determining factors are future occurrences. The future can mean tomorrow, next year, or even five or more years from now.

Unfortunately, managers must make decisions today that are to be in effect tomorrow. A new-product decision which must be made today will be affected by future demand. A choice among alternative methods for acquiring capital will be affected by future interest rates and the availability of funds. If we could delay the decision until all the factors affecting the results were known, we would be too late. I would be very happy to buy stock in Corporation X today if I were absolutely certain that the price of the stock would go up tomorrow. Unfortunately, the future behavior of stock prices is uncertain. If I defer my buy-or-not-buy decision until I know tomorrow's price, I will be too late to benefit from the increase if it does occur.

Uncertainty is a fact of life for managers. Managers who know how to deal with it will be successful because their decisions will take its effects into account. Managers who are incapable of dealing with uncertainty will be stymied. Either they will not make the necessary decisions at all because they are always waiting for the uncertainties to be resolved or they will make poor decisions because they don't know how to cope with the uncertainties.

Fortunately, there are simple techniques for dealing with uncertainty in decision making. These techniques do not guarantee that every decision will be a good one. They do, however, guarantee that in the long run the number of good decisions will far exceed the number of bad ones. Remember, a successful manager doesn't have to be right all the time, only most of the time.

FORMAL INTUITIVE DECISION MAKING

What can good intuitive decision makers do well that poor intuitive decision makers cannot do? The answer is that they can process and integrate information. Managers are continuously inundated with all kinds of information. Some of it is valuable and some of it is useless. The information may be received verbally or in writing, or it simply may be observed. It may be submitted formally, as in a report, or informally in conversation. A great deal of the information may be redundant. The good intuitive decision maker is able to sort and classify this information, distinguish among the valuable, the worthless, and the redundant, assign values and priorities, and integrate the whole into an accurate picture of the decision situation.

It is very difficult to perform these functions entirely by intuition. Some systematic procedure is needed. The degree of difficulty increases tremendously as the amount of information increases. That is why there are so few good intuitive decision makers and also why a manager who is a good decision maker at a low level of management may fail miserably at some higher level. Not only are the decisions more numerous and more important at the higher management levels, but the sheer amount of information that must be considered at these levels can be overwhelming.

It is the uncommon manager who can consistently make good high-level decisions intuitively. Most need help. Chester Barnard, former president of New Jersey Bell Telephone Co. and the Rockefeller Foundation, notes in his book *The Functions of the Executive** that managers generally try to avoid making decisions. He adds that their capacity to make decisions is quite narrow, although it can be developed by training and experience. However, before there can be training there must be a method.

The good intuitive decision maker is like someone with a photographic memory. He has a gift. Most of us do not have that gift. Without a photographic memory we must resort to hard work in order to memorize the facts that are important and necessary to us. Similarly, without the ability to make good intuitive decisions, we must work hard to master techniques for improving our skill. These techniques do not have to be very difficult. Nor must we be mathematicians to master them. All that is required is some time, a little effort, and the desire to become a good decision maker and a successful manager.

A recent television news program included a tongue-in-cheek commentary on rating systems. The best rating system, the speaker remarked, consists in rating everything on a scale of 1 to 10. Such a system can be used for rating anything from food to music to television news announcers. And the best thing about such a rating system is that it makes decision making easy. Once the ratings are assigned, the rater can make decisions—that is, choices—without having to think much about them.

There is much truth in this wry comment. A simple procedure of rating alternatives is a useful tool for decision making. It is easy to do, it is effective, and best of all it doesn't require a knowledge of mathematics. As a decision-making technique, it utilizes assessments based on subjective rather than objective

* Cambridge, Mass.: Harvard University Press, 1967.

information in the possession of the decision maker. In addition, it forces the decision maker to use this information in a systematic manner. We will discuss this and other simple methods for intuitive decision making in subsequent chapters.

WHAT IS A MANAGERIAL DECISION?

What is the difference between a managerial decision and those common everyday decisions made by managers and non-managers alike? Managerial decisions are complex decisions that have a significant effect on some organization. In business organizations, the effect of managerial decisions is generally monetary—that is, it is measured in dollars and cents. The crux of the definition of managerial lies in the complexity of the decision situation and the significance of the result to the organization. Of course, terms such as complexity and significance are relative. A $10,000 loss may be insignificant to a large corporation but could lead to bankruptcy for a small family business. We make the distinction between managerial and nonmanagerial decisions simply to eliminate the trivial or unimportant. For example, a decision about carrying an umbrella when the weather bureau predicts rain or a decision about what to wear to a dinner party would not normally be considered a managerial decision. But who can tell? Under certain circumstances even decisions such as these might have significant consequences to the organization.

2

THE STRUCTURE
OF MANAGERIAL DECISIONS

Managerial decision situations differ in many ways. They may differ with different types of organizations—for example, an oil company versus a department store. They may differ as to the organizational function involved—that is, production decisions, purchasing decisions, marketing decisions, investment decisions, and so on. They may differ as to their relative importance or uniqueness, or as to the time frame over which the effects will be apparent. However, there are certain factors that are common to all decision situations. Before any general decision-making techniques can be formulated, these common factors must be identified and understood.

A decision is a choice. More precisely, a decision is a choice among alternative courses of action that lead to some desired result. Without alternatives there can be no decision. Without alternatives, there is only one course of action available; consequently, no choice can or need be made. Keep in mind, however, that taking no action is a legitimate alternative. That is, a choice can be made between some positive act and the status quo. This is still a decision situation.

Because a decision involves a choice that leads to some specific result, the decision maker must be aware of all the possible consequences that could result from choosing a specific act. In other words, the decision maker must always ask this question: "If I select this particular act from the set of alternative acts available, what will the consequences be?"

If each possible act has a single, unequivocal, and certain outcome, then the decision problem is relatively simple. For even though the various outcomes must be valued in some way, preferably in quantitative terms, a choice can be made by comparing these single and certain outcomes and selecting the act that leads to the best result for that particular decision situation. Such a decision situation is called *decision making under certainty*.

Unfortunately, most decision situations are not that simple. Generally, the choice of an act does not lead to a single, certain outcome. The consequence of selecting an act is usually uncertain. Therefore, in order to make effective decisions, the decision maker must take uncertainty into account.

In order to deal with uncertainty, the decision maker must first determine what causes it. In other words, he must find out where the uncertainty comes from. There is no uncertainty associated with the set of available acts. These alternatives either exist or they do not. The uncertainty in the decision situation is associated with the consequences. This is what makes the choice of an act difficult. However, it should be apparent that the consequences do not *cause* the uncertainty. The uncertainty stems from some other factor which we have not yet identified.

For any one of the alternative acts available to the decision maker under uncertainty, there can be several consequences. For example, a decision to market a new product could result in any one of the following consequences: (1) profit, (2) breakeven, or (3) loss. This is, of course, a gross simplification. There could, in fact, be many other possible consequences associated with that particular act. However, whether that act results in profit, breakeven, or loss depends upon various factors beyond the control of the decision maker. Some of these factors are the presence or absence of competition, the costs associated with marketing the product, and the demand for the product at various prices.

In the language of decision making, these uncontrollable factors are called the *states of the world* or the *states of nature*. The uncertainty in any decision situation stems from these states of nature. If the marketing decision maker knew that there would be no competition, knew the exact cost of marketing the product, and knew exactly what the demand for the product would be, then the situation would become decision making under certainty. The solution would be straightforward. The decision maker would simply determine the profit or payoff under each of the alternatives and select the act for which the payoff was best.

However, in most managerial decision situations, as in the one described above, the decision maker can never be absolutely certain about the states of nature. He cannot be sure of the number of competitors he will encounter or even whether there will be any competitors. Costs of all kinds are never completely known in advance, and they change frequently. The future demand for the product is probably the least certain of all these factors. Nevertheless, in order to make a decision, the decision maker must recognize and deal with this uncertainty in some systematic manner.

Statisticians and mathematicians have developed a theory for dealing with decision making under uncertainty. This decision theory is quite complex and difficult to apply in practical situations, and it requires considerable knowledge of mathematics and statistics. The theory is therefore somewhat impractical for the typical business decision-making situation. We will, however, adopt some of the principles of the theory, simplify others, and derive some new techniques in order to construct a decision-making procedure that is practical, applicable to most managerial decision situations, and relatively easy to use.

DECISION COMPONENTS

We have already noted the three major componets of any decision situation: (1) alternative acts, (2) states of nature, and (3) consequences. Of primary concern to the decision maker is the component of consequences. However, consequences are determined by the joint effect of the two other components. That is, the consequences result from the choice of an act by the decision maker and the choice of a state by nature. It may be helpful to think of each component in terms of who or what has control. For example, the decision maker has total control over only one of the three components—the acts. The decision maker alone can choose one of the acts. The states of nature are determined by outside factors and are totally beyond the control of the decision maker. The consequences of each act are jointly controlled by nature and the decision maker.

We can think of the decision-making process as follows: the decision maker chooses an act, nature chooses a state, and some specific consequence results. For each combination of act and state of nature, there is some specific consequence. This consequence is called a *conditional consequence,* since it depends on which state nature chooses. Each act has a set of conditional consequences associated with it, one for each of the possible states of nature. The decision maker's uncertainty about the state of nature is reflected by his uncertainty about which of the conditional consequences will result after he has selected a particular act.

The relationship among acts, states, and conditional consequences is shown in Figure 2.1. The alternative acts are listed across the top of the table and are identified by the symbols a_1, a_2, a_3, and so on. The possible states of nature are listed in the extreme left-hand column and are identified by the symbols s_1, s_2, s_3, and so on. Under the column associated with the first act, a_1, are a series of conditional consequences. For example, conditional consequence 11, or cc_{11}, is the consequence associated with a_1 and s_1. Conditional consequence 12, or cc_{12}, is the consequence associated with a_1 and s_2. The other conditional consequences are numbered in the same way, with the first number corresponding to an act and the second number corresponding to a particular state.

Displays such as Figure 2.1 are frequently referred to as payoff tables. The payoffs for an act and the various states of nature correspond to the conditional consequences of the act. Payoff tables are a useful device for visualizing all the components of the decision situation in a concise and compact manner.

FIGURE 2.1   Relationship among acts, states, and conditional consequences.

STATES	ACTS				
	a_1	a_2	a_3	a_4	. . .
s_1	cc_{11}	cc_{21}	cc_{31}	cc_{41}	. . .
s_2	cc_{12}	cc_{22}	cc_{32}	cc_{42}	. . .
s_3	cc_{13}	cc_{23}	cc_{33}	cc_{43}	. . .
s_4	cc_{14}	cc_{24}	cc_{34}	cc_{44}	. . .
.	.	.	.	.	
.	.	.	.	.	
.	.	.	.	.	
.	.	.	.	.	

Another graphic device for displaying the components of the decision situation is the decision tree. Payoff tables and decision trees are discussed in more detail in Chapter 4.

STATES OF NATURE

The consequences of any action on the part of a decision maker are dependent upon certain factors which are beyond his control. These factors are referred to as the *states of nature*. The term "state of nature" is not necessarily limited to nature in the ordinary sense of the word. It is a general term which includes all those factors beyond the control of the decision maker that affect the outcome of a decision. In addition to actual states of nature—floods, storms, droughts, and so on—it encompasses such factors as the prices of raw materials, the availability and cost of labor, interest rates, and the acts of other individuals.

For example, a farmer's decision to plant a particular crop will be affected by the amount of rainfall over the next growing season. This decision will also be affected by the expressed preferences of many individuals for different types of foodstuffs, which in turn will affect the demand for the farmer's product and the price at which he can sell it. In this case, the factors affecting this farmer's decision consist of an actual state of nature, rainfall, and a sort of pseudo-state of nature, the demand for the product.

Similarly, a manufacturer's decision to market a new product may be affected by the decision of a competitor on marketing a similar product. The competitor may deliberately make a decision that will have an adverse effect on this particular manufacturer. The goal may be to force this manufacturer out of business or to cause him to lose money in order to create a market situation more beneficial to the competitor. In this case the state of nature bearing on the manufacturer's decision is the conscious act of a competitor whose goals are directly in opposition to his own.

The state of nature in the previous example is the occurrence or lack of occurrence of a particular event—that is, the competitor markets the product or he doesn't. Such a state of nature is said to be dichotomous: it has only two values. On the other hand, for the farmer's decision the state of nature could assume numerous values. Rainfall over the growing season could range, say, between 18 and 36 inches. Each increment of rainfall would have a different effect on the harvest. The demand for the product as reflected in the market price per bushel could also vary, and just as widely. In each case there could be multiple states of nature.

In many practical decision situations the number of possible states of nature may be so great as to make analysis of the problem almost insurmountable. It is usually necessary, therefore, to reduce the states of nature to a reasonable number. This is generally done by eliminating those states whose effect on the decision consequences is determined to be minimal and retaining only those factors that appear to have a significant effect.

The elimination of inconsequential states of nature is an important part of the decision procedure and is based primarily on the judgment of the decision maker. However, eliminating states of nature prematurely can be dangerous. All possible states of nature should be listed in formulating and describing the decision situation. Then the effect of each state on every act should be determined or estimated. All of these data should be tabulated, preferably in the form of a payoff table. Only then can the effects of a particular state of nature be compared with the effects of other states, and their significance be assessed.

Both judgment and analysis must be exercised by the decision maker in this procedure.

VALUING CONSEQUENCES

Under conditions of uncertainty, where each possible act has a single certain consequence, a decision can be made simply by comparing the consequences of all the acts and selecting the one that has the most beneficial result. However, even under conditions of certainty, before any consequences can be compared they should be expressed in terms of some common unit of value. It is simple enough to state the consequences of an act in words. For example:

"Improve recognition of the company's trademark."
"Enhance the company's reputation as an innovator."
"Increase customer goodwill."

However, it is virtually impossible to compare the value of consequences so stated. Unless the consequences can be converted to some common unit of value and expressed in terms of numbers, such comparisons are meaningless.

Fortunately, most managerial decisions, particularly in business and industry, can be valued in dollars and cents. Whether the operational unit affected is a retail store, a department in a manufacturing organization, or the corporate entity itself, the consequences of most decisions can be measured in terms of dollars of cost or loss, or dollars of profit or gain.

For example, the consequences of an advertising decision can be measured in terms of increased sales in dollars. Of course, it is also possible to measure the sales increase in terms of units of product sold. However, there is obviously a direct relationship between units and dollars, and the conversion from one unit to the other is simple. The consequence of a capital equipment purchasing decision can be measured in terms of return on investment or reduction in cost, also easily expressed in dollars and cents.

Is monetary value *always* an adequate measure of consequences? No. There are some decision situations that involve social consequences and require answers to questions like these:

"What is a human life worth?"
"What is the monetary value of a cure for cancer or the rehabilitation of a habitual criminal?"

Decisions involving such social consequences are much more common in government than they are in business organizations. Nevertheless, even in business, dollars and cents may not always reflect the value of consequences adequately. The units used in any value system should have constant value. However, the value of a dollar to a decision maker or an organization depends on circumstances. As noted in the previous chapter, a $10,000 loss may be insignificant to a large corporation but could lead to bankruptcy for a small family business. Consequently, a decision maker will place different values on the dollar, depending on the number of dollars involved in the decision situation and the financial condition of the organization at the time.

When monetary value is clearly not a satisfactory measure of consequences, some other numerical value system should be devised. One such system is based on the concept of utility, a subject of much research and many books. We will not discuss this theory here, since situations in business where it might be required are very rare. In most business decisions, monetary value is an adequate measure of consequences and we will limit ourselves to such decision situations in this book.

DECISION CRITERIA

In order to compare the consequences of several available acts, a decision maker needs to have some criterion for determining which is better or best. In decisions under certainty, where each act is associated with one and only one consequence, the criterion can be a very simple one. For example:

"Select the act that results in the highest profit."
"Select the least-cost alternative."

If the alternatives are valued numerically in terms of dollars of profit or cost, then the selection of an act under one of these criteria is straightforward. The act with either the highest or the lowest numerically valued consequence would be selected, depending on whether the consequences were valued in terms of profit or cost.

Under uncertainty, things are not quite so simple. Each act can have several conditional consequences, as determined by the prevailing state of nature. Usually, no single act is best for all possible states of nature and, of course, the states of nature are uncertain. Nevertheless, the decision maker must have some criterion on which to base his choice of an act.

Various criteria can be used as a decision strategy under uncertainty. The choice of some specific criterion should be based on the objectives of the organization and on the decision maker's subjective judgments about the uncertain states of nature. Even in the most highly sophisticated mathematical decision models the choice of a decision criterion results from the judgment of the decision maker, and any final decision is dependent as much on the criterion used as it is on the mathematics of the model and the data input. A poor choice of criterion can negate the effects of the most sophisticated mathematical model.

The informal intuitive decision maker frequently does not articulate the criterion used in making his decision. He may not even be aware that the criterion has a name and a formal structure and has very probably been described in numerous books on decision making. For example, managers frequently select a course of action that in their judgment has the greatest likelihood of maximizing some measure of economic gain. Or under different circumstances, they may select the act that they believe has the greatest likelihood of minimizing loss. Under the appropriate conditions, these are both reasonable criteria and have been formally characterized by the names *maximax* and *minimax*. (See Chapter 5.) There are also other criteria which are based on average or expected gains or losses. However, all the various decision criteria have this in common: they require some assessment by the decision maker of the likelihood of occurrence of the various states of nature that bear on the decision situation—that is, they require judgments either explicitly or implicitly about uncertainty. We will discuss the various decision-making criteria in Chapter 4 and show how a manager should select the criterion that will produce the best results under various conditions of uncertainty.

PROGRAMMABLE AND UNPROGRAMMABLE DECISIONS

The decision situations faced by a typical manager may be either programmable or unprogrammable. A programmable decision situation is one that is repetitive or recurring. When a decision situation recurs with some frequency, a general solution can usually be found and used over and over again. This relieves the decision maker of the burden of going through the decision-making procedure whenever that particular problem arises.

A good example of a programmable decision is the inventory reorder problem. When inventory is depleted as materials or products are used, decisions must be made regarding when and how much to reorder. Furthermore, these decision situations recur frequently for the same inventory item. Problems of this type are called reorder point and economic order quantity (EOQ) problems. The objective of reorder decisions is to minimize total cost, which consists of the cost of placing the order and the cost of carrying inventory. However, a new decision need not be evaluated and made every time the inventory of this particular material is depleted. There are mathematical methods for determining the reorder point and the frequency and size of orders that will minimize the total cost. Thus, once a solution is achieved for this problem, a system can be established for carrying out the appropriate action whenever the situation arises.

The most important and difficult type of decision the manager faces is the unprogrammable decision. This is the one-of-a-kind situation that will never recur in exactly the same way but nevertheless contains those components common to all decision situations. No general solution can be applied to unprogrammable decision situations; however, a general *procedure* can be formulated. It is this procedure that we will begin to develop here.

A FORMAL INTUITIVE DECISION PROCESS

The intuitive decision maker, consciously or unconsciously, follows a logical process of thought and evaluation in arriving at a decision. This process will be formalized and presented in the following chapters, together with a set of tools needed to make it work. Briefly, the formal intuitive decision-making process includes the following general stages:

1. Identifying and listing the complete set of viable alternative acts that are available to the decision maker under a particular decision situation.
2. Identifying and listing the set of states of nature that have an appreciable effect on the consequences of the acts.
3. Determining and valuing the conditional consequences of each act for every state of nature.
4. Eliminating states of nature that have insignificant effects and acts that are clearly inferior to other available acts.
5. Selecting the appropriate decision criterion in light of the organization's objectives and the decision maker's subjective assessment of the uncertainties pertaining to the situation.
6. Quantifying the uncertainties in terms of the likelihood or probability that a particular state of nature will occur.
7. Using the quantitative measure of uncertainty, the conditional consequences, and the decision criterion to choose the optimal act.

The tools that are required to carry out this procedure are primarily judgment and common sense. Formal procedures include organizing, ranking, counting, estimating, and simple arithmetic. Some simple tables, which are included in the appendix, will also be required.

PROBLEM SOLVING AND DECISION MAKING

What is the relationship between problem solving and decision making? Quite frequently, the two terms are used interchangeably in business decision situations.

Problem solving and decision making are not synonymous. However, decision making involves problem solving and, at least in business, problem solving always leads to some decision. The process of selecting a particular course of action from a set of alternatives is itself a problem, and many times a difficult one. But more than this, decisions are the end result of a problem-solving process. In business, decision making is neither a game nor an intellectual exercise. The same can be said of problem solving. Problems result from attempts to achieve the goals of the organization. Problems must be solved if those goals are to be attained. But solutions by themselves do not achieve goals. It is the decisions resulting from these solutions that achieve goals.

For example, if the problem involves public acceptance of a new product or customer reaction to a proposed advertising campaign, the solution to the problem should lead to a decision to act in some manner. Either market the product or don't market it. Either implement the proposed advertising program or scrap it. Without such a decision, the problem solution is worthless. Consequently, problem solving and decision making go hand in hand. Any procedure that covers one of these without the other is bound to be unsatisfactory. In the following chapter, some common and not so common problem-solving and decision-making techniques are described.

3

OTHER DECISION-MAKING
AND PROBLEM-SOLVING TECHNIQUES

Before we proceed with a discussion of formal intuitive decision making, it might be informative to examine some other decision-making and problem-solving methods that many managers use or are being taught through books, seminars, and training sessions. With the exception of informal intuitive decision making, which is not really a technique at all, most of the methods described here are problem-solving rather than decision-making procedures. Some of these methods seek to stimulate creativity in generating new ideas. Others attempt to solve problems by examining them from new or unorthodox perspectives. Only one, the quantitative-mathematical approach, called *statistical decision theory*, attempts to provide decisions or solutions that are optimal according to some objective criterion. In that respect it is the only satisfactory method for improving the manager's decision-making ability in a measurable way. Nevertheless, several of the other techniques have been used in problem solving with good results and are worthwhile discussing.

INFORMAL INTUITIVE DECISION MAKING

Informal intuitive decision making is a term that describes how most managers make decisions. Many people might claim that managers, like bettors on horse races, play their hunches. Even managers themselves might characterize their decision-making techniques this way. How many times have you made a decision with the thought, "I just have a feeling this is the thing to do," or "Something tells me this will work"?

Hunch, intuition, and just plain gut feeling usually have some logical basis. In the course of their schooling, early work experience, and managerial experience, managers have been exposed to a large amount of data on the operating factors in their environment. Much of these data have been absorbed and stored in the managers' minds, along with a set of personal operating principles—rules for processing and evaluating the data. With each new decision situation, more information is added to the data bank. Frequently, the operating rules are modified as the results of previous decisions become known. Each decision situation stimulates the manager to process new data in accordance with his personal operating rules. This procedure, when performed subconsciously, leads to hunches and good or bad feelings about specific factors in the decision situation.

Of course, with no objective procedures and criteria, a manager's decision-making performance will only be as good as his inherent ability to process information and to formulate effective operating rules. Some managers are better at doing this than others. Most improve with experience. But with few exceptions, decision-making performance based on intuition is erratic and inconsistent. Consequently, managers and management theorists are continuously trying to establish objective procedures that will result in consistently good or optimal decisions. In other words, they are trying to formalize the intuitive process.

For the very successful manager whose informal intuitive decision making has always been first rate, there is no reason to believe that it will not continue at that level. Since an axiom of human behavior holds that we should not tamper with something that works, it might be unwise for these good decision makers to attempt to change their ways. However, for the large majority whose decision-making performance has been erratic and inconsistent and averages out near the 50% level, something more is certainly needed.

CHECKLISTING

One of the most common and simple decision techniques is checklisting. Checklisting involves the preparation of an exhaustive list of factors that bear on the results of the decision. All or most of these factors must be positive for a specific alternative to be selected.

Checklists are most useful in go/no-go situations—that is, situations where there are only two alternatives, one of which entails some positive action on the part of the decision maker or his organization. A typical use of checklisting occurs in the cockpit of every jet transport plane before takeoff. The flight crew goes over a lengthy list of items that must be checked off before a decision can be made to take off.

Sometimes a checklist is referred to as a countdown. Mission control officers prepare a lengthy checklist which must be counted down before a decision can be made to launch a missile or rocket. The alternatives in these decision situations are either launch or abort the mission.

Similar situations occur in business when a manager must decide whether to manufacture and market a new product or shelve the project; to accept a contract or reject it; to expand facilities or simply maintain the present ones. For each of these decision situations a checklist of factors that should be favorable to the "go" decision can be compiled and checked off as each is investigated. For example, a checklist for a decision on a production contract might include the following items:

Contract price and payment schedule.
Direct costs.
Indirect costs.
Availability of required facilities.
Availability of required labor skills.
Availability of required capital.
Required completion schedule.
Customer's acceptance procedures for finished material.
Nature of penalty clause if any.

As each item is investigated and determined to be favorable, it is checked off the list. If all items are positive, a go decision can be made. If one or more items are unfavorable, a no-go decision may be indicated. Of course, since decision situations vary, the number of unfavorable items required for a no-go decision will also vary. Some decision rule must be established for determining the number of unfavorable items that could occur and still lead to a go decision.

Checklisting can be very helpful to managers when the decision situation is a relatively simple, two-alternative problem. It forces the decision maker to examine the decision situation in detail, investigating all the factors that bear on the decision. It systematizes what otherwise might be overlooked. Checklisting is much less helpful when the decision is complex. For example, when more than two alternatives are available, the checklist does not indicate which of the several alternatives is superior to the others, and it may even be confusing to the manager.

Another limitation of the checklist is that it makes no provision for weighting the various factors according to their importance. This may not be a significant drawback for the jet pilot in making a takeoff decision, since the failure of any item on the list to check out as satisfactory is sufficient to abort the mission. However, most business decisions are not that straightforward. All factors on a checklist are not necessarily of equal importance to the decision outcome. A checklist cannot indicate that fact.

RATING OR PRIORITY SYSTEMS

As noted in Chapter 1, a rating system in which alternatives are ranked according to some criterion of value can be a simple and effective decision-making tool. Once such a system has been established, it can be used repeatedly for making choices until some new alternative enters the system or a change occurs that requires a reevaluation of priorities.

For example, an appliance manufacturer may purchase parts needed in the manufacturing process from several different suppliers. Each time a particular part is reordered, a decision must be made on which supplier to use. Each supplier represents an alternative source for the parts; consequently, the selection of a supplier from the set of alternatives constitutes a decision.

It should not be necessary to evaluate each alternative—that is, every supplier—each time a new order is placed. If the suppliers can be ranked from best to worst according to some criterion such as price, quality, delivery, and so on, or some combination of these factors, then the selection process becomes very simple. The manufacturer's purchasing agent can start at the top of the list and choose suppliers in order, moving down the list only when a preferred supplier cannot accept or fill the entire order.

A rating system could also be used in deciding which customer orders to fill when insufficient merchandise is available. Or it could be used by a manufacturer to allocate limited resources to different product lines. In the first of these cases, a priority system of customers could be established on the basis of value to the manufacturer, and the orders filled by beginning at the top and working down the list. For example, customers might be ranked according to the size of their orders. Then the orders would be filled beginning with the largest and working toward the smallest until the merchandise was depleted. In the second case, a priority ranking of products could be established according to some criterion such as profit margin. In other words, scarce resources would be assigned to the manufacture of each product, beginning with the product having the highest profit margin, proceeding to the one with the next highest, and so on. For example, an oil company might allocate supplies of crude oil to the processing of premium gasoline, regular gasoline, and unleaded gasoline in that order.

A rating or priority system can be useful in making programmable decisions—those that recur with some frequency. Such a system is not likely to be applicable to nonprogrammable (one-of-a-kind) decisions, simply because the conditions surrounding these decisions are unique. Since nonprogrammable decisions are usually the most important and certainly the most difficult ones that managers make, a rating system is not, by itself, a powerful enough tool in these cases. However, as part of a broader and more comprehensive decision-making procedure, a rating system is a useful technique.

MORPHOLOGICAL ANALYSIS

Morphological analysis stresses the discovery of fundamental patterns or relationships among ideas. This is done by arranging ideas into a display called a morphological chart or *morphologram*. The chart consists of many columns, each labeled with one of the parameters of the problem. In morphology, a *parameter* is a constant whose value varies with the circumstances of its application. More broadly, a parameter is a characteristic of the problem situation. Under each parameter is listed an exhaustive set of possible values. An extremely large number of relationships can be determined by combining each parameter value with every other parameter value in the chart. For example, if there are four parameters to the problem and each parameter has eight possible values, there would be $8 \times 8 \times 8 \times 8 = 4,096$ different relationships.

Since most new ideas are the result of combining other ideas, morphology proposes that a systematic procedure for combining ideas will provide insights into a problem that would not otherwise be apparent. This association of ideas is called *synthesis*. According to the principles of morphological analysis, the ultimate requirement for making good decisions is a clear and comprehensive view of the overall decision situation. The morphological chart is a tool to provide such a comprehensive view.

It is conceivable that after all the parameters of a problem and their possible values have been specified, the total number of possible relationships will be so large as to preclude detailed analysis. In such a case, one or two of the most important parameters are identified and the least important ones eliminated. In this manner, the number of possible relationships is made amenable to analysis. This process of identifying parameters and then rating them utilizes a priority system. This type of procedure is common in all true decision-making systems.

The decision-making capabilities of morphological analysis are debatable. Supposedly, the system recognizes that the chief responsibility of a manager is to make decisions and the principal responsibility of everyone else is to provide the manager with the material necessary for making the decision. However, aside from the morphological chart, the decision-making technique itself is vague and indefinite. For example, in morphological analysis a good decision is defined as one which provides a workable solution to a problem and is acceptable to those affected by it. Such a definition may lead to a workable decision, but it is not sufficient in itself to produce a good decision much less a "best" decision. Effective managers are not satisfied with workable solutions; they are concerned with finding the best solutions.

BRAINSTORMING

Are two heads always better than one and three always better than two? Is the total problem-solving ability of several people greater than the sum of their individual abilities? Confirmed brainstormers would answer yes to both questions.

Brainstorming was developed in the early 1960s by Alex Osborn in his book *Applied Imagination.** Brainstorming, also called *creative problem solving*, attempts to find new alternatives for solving problems in a group setting by freeing the imaginations of the participants and encouraging them to build on the ideas generated by others. No idea is too esoteric, too eccentric, or too wild to be excluded from consideration.

The aim of a brainstorming session is to generate as many ideas as possible with the hope that out of the multitude, one or two will have some value. The brainstorming environment is free and unstructured. Members of the group are encouraged to say anything that comes into their minds. In a sense, a brainstorming session is like a free-association test, often used in psychological counseling sessions.

Fundamental to brainstorming is the concept of synergistic action. This, as Osborn explains in his book, is the idea that two or more things can be combined to yield something greater than the sum of the individual parts. Brainstorming relies on the synergistic action among group members to produce a result that is greater than could have occurred had the individual members been working on the problem separately. Brainstorming sessions

* New York: Charles Scribner's Sons, 1963.

have been conducted with groups containing as many as 200 members and as few as 4. An ideal size has never been established, but it is generally assumed that the best size is about 12 members, including a chairman and a co-chairman.

A brainstorming session begins when a specific problem has been selected for the group to work on. The group leader usually supplies a short description of the problem to the group a day or two before the scheduled meeting. When the brainstorming session begins, the chairman again explains the problem and calls for suggestions from the group. If the suggestions are slow in coming or cease, the leader may get them started again by contributing ideas of his own.

Every idea suggested by the group is recorded by a secretary. The list of suggestions is screened and evaluated at a later meeting, usually by conferees who were not part of the original brainstorming group. During the session, certain rules are established in order to stimulate the flow of ideas and to avoid inhibiting members from expressing them. These rules are:

1. Criticism is out. No judgment or evaluation of any idea is to be made during the brainstorming session.
2. Free-wheeling is encouraged. No idea is too wild or absurd to be suggested.
3. Quantity is desirable. The greater the number of suggestions, the more likely that something useful will result.
4. Combination of ideas and improvement on previous suggestions are encouraged.

By encouraging group members to add to and develop ideas suggested by other members, the concept of association operates. Every idea suggested can stimulate the creation of new and additional ideas.

A brainstorming panel has completed its job when it has submitted a screened list of ideas. There is certainly no guarantee that any of the ideas so generated will lead to a viable solution to the problem. Furthermore, nothing that the brainstorming panel does can be construed as decision making. After the panel has met, a decision must be made by someone as to which if any of the ideas are to be implemented. The brainstorming panel makes no such decision.

Brainstorming, like several other techniques mentioned in this chapter, is a problem-solving rather than a decision-making procedure. Even in problem solving, however, its goal is limited. Brainstorming is a method for generating ideas or alternatives. If lack of alternatives is the main problem, then brainstorming could be a problem-solving technique. However, since decision making requires that a choice be made among alternatives and nothing in the brainstorming procedure addresses itself to how such a choice should be made, it cannot be characterized as a decision-making procedure.

If brainstorming is not a decision-making technique, is it even effective as a problem-solving technique? That is, does it accomplish its goal at a lower cost, in terms of resources committed, than some other method? In a typical brainstorming session, 10 to 15 people meet for 45 to 60 minutes. This means that a total of 7.5 to 15 man-hours of effort are expended per session to generate a list of ideas, most of which will turn out to be useless. It is likely that a directed discussion between two or three knowledgeable professionals could produce better solutions in less time and with greater efficiency. As Bernard Benson noted in his 1957 article,* no amount of cerebral popcorn will produce the optimum solution to a complicated problem or provide a substitute for systematic reasoning.

SYNECTICS

Synectics (a word derived from the Greek) means the joining together of different and apparently irrelevant elements. The emphasis in synectics is on creativity—that is, on generating creative solutions to problems. In the sense that it uses groups to generate new ideas, it is similar to brainstorming. However, whereas brainstorming attempts to find a few worthwhile ideas by creating a climate in which a large quantity of suggestions can be generated, synectics attempts to find a solution by looking at the problem in new and previously unthought-of ways. This is done by attempting to make the strange familiar and the familiar strange.

* Bernard Benson, "Let's Toss This Idea Up," *Fortune,* October 1957.

William J. Gordon, in his book *Synectics,** divides the creative process into the following nine phases:

1. *Problem as given.* Before participants work on a solution, a detailed statement of the problem must be formulated.

2. *The strange made familiar.* No matter how commonplace the problem, a concentrated analysis will reveal elements that have not previously been apparent. This phase brings hidden aspects of the problem into the open.

3. *Problem as understood.* Every facet of the problem is isolated and analyzed in detail.

4. *Operational mechanisms.* Analogies are developed for a better understanding of the problem.

5. *The familiar made strange.* Through the analogies developed previously, the problem as understood is seen in a way not considered previously.

6. *Psychological states.* The participants enter a psychological climate of involvement, detachment, and speculation which is conducive to creative problem solving.

7. *States integrated with problem.* The most pertinent analogies are conceptually compared with the problem as understood.

8. *Viewpoint.* The comparison of analogies with the problem as understood results in a new and different viewpoint. When the comparison is effective, it provides a new technical insight into the problem.

9. *Solution or research target.* The viewpoint is reduced to practice. If new material needs development, the viewpoint may become the subject of further research.

In essence, synectics is an attempt to stimulate creative solutions through group interactions. It differs from brainstorming in that the group is generally smaller and consists of individuals specially selected for their expertise in areas that might bear on the problem. Although the approach is more reasoned and structured than brainstorming, it too is geared to problem solutions rather than to decisions. Consequently, although synectics may produce a solution to some previously intractable problem,

* New York: Harper & Row, 1961.

it still does not help the decision maker, since it provides no procedure for selecting the best of several alternatives.

THE DELPHI METHOD

The Delphi method is another attempt to achieve creative solutions to problems by using groups of experts. Delphi is a method of structuring group communication in such a way as to make it effective in providing solutions to complex problems. The key word here is "structuring." Delphi is a much more highly structured procedure than either brainstorming or synectics. The Delphi structure provides for the feedback of individual contributions, the assessment of group judgments, opportunities to revise previously stated views, and a degree of anonymity for the participants.

There are two forms of the Delphi process. The first, called conventional Delphi, involves a small monitor team. This team designs a questionnaire which is sent to a larger group of respondents. After the questionnaire is completed and returned, the monitor team summarizes the responses and, based on the results, prepares and sends a new questionnaire to the participants. The procedure continues until a solution is achieved. The second form of Delphi, called real-time Delphi, replaces the monitor team to a large degree with a computer. The computer compiles the results of the questionnaire responses, thus eliminating the delay created when the monitor team must prepare the summary manually.

The four phases of a Delphi procedure include exploration, understanding, reconciliation, and evaluation. In the exploration phase, each participant contributes information which he feels is pertinent to the problem. In the second phase, the monitor team attempts to understand how the respondent group views the problem—that is, where the members agree and where they disagree. If significant disagreement exists, the third phase is initiated to uncover the reasons for the differences and reconcile them. In the final phase, all previously gathered information is analyzed and the evaluation is fed back to respondents for consideration.

The major difference between Delphi and other group problem-solving methods is that the respondents never meet face to face. All the communication between group members is remote. The isolation of group members and the remote communication become desirable under the following conditions:

1. More people are needed in the group than can effectively interact in a face-to-face exchange.
2. Time and cost make frequent group meetings impractical.
3. Disagreements among group members are so severe that communication must be refereed and anonymity ensured.
4. Face-to-face meetings could result in the dominance of certain viewpoints by sheer weight of numbers or strength of personality.

Like synectics, Delphi is based primarily on expert opinions. Also, like synectics, it is a method for bringing these opinions to bear on some problem and to reach agreement or at least consensus on a solution. However, it is not decision making and consequently fails to help the manager who is confronted with a situation requiring a choice. In that respect, Delphi has the same weaknesses and shortcomings as all the other methods discussed so far.

KEPNER–TREGOE

Charles Kepner and Benjamin Tregoe, in their book *The Rational Manager,** attempt to provide a systematic approach to both problem solving and decision making that the practicing manager will find valuable. Kepner and Tregoe make a definite distinction between problem analysis (getting to the cause of the problem) and decision making (deciding what to do about it). However, they add that the difficulties underlying both problem analysis and decision making are so interrelated that an understanding of both is necessary if a manager is to use information efficiently. And information, they go on to state, is the raw material of management.

Kepner and Tregoe identify seven basic concepts in problem

* New York: McGraw-Hill, 1965.

analysis and seven in decision making. These fourteen concepts comprise a two-part cycle which includes both the problem-solving and decision-making aspects of a decision situation. These concepts are:

Problem solving
1. There is a standard against which actual performance can be measured.
2. A problem is a deviation from the standard.
3. A deviation must be identified, located, and described.
4. A distinction can be made between that which has been affected by the cause and that which has not.
5. The cause of a problem (deviation from standard) is a change that has taken place through some mechanism or condition.
6. Possible causes can be deduced from the relevant changes observed.
7. The most likely cause is one that explains all the facts specified in the problem.

Decision making
1. The objective of a decision must be specified.
2. Objectives are classified according to their importance.
3. Alternative actions are specified.
4. Every alternative is evaluated for the extent to which it meets the objectives.
5. The alternative best able to achieve all the objectives is chosen as a tentative decision.
6. The tentative decision is explored for possible adverse consequences.
7. Any possible effects of a final decision are controlled by taking other actions to prevent their occurrence.

According to Kepner and Tregoe, problem solving involves finding an explanation for the observed deviation from the standard. This explanation can be verified, because the event or cause has already occurred. Decision making, on the other hand, involves a choice among various ways of accomplishing an objective. Selecting the best of several possible alternatives is the end of the decision-making process. However, once the decision is made, some action must be taken. It is impossible to verify by observation that the decision was optimal until the required action has been taken and the consequences of that action are known; that is, have the deviations been corrected?

In order to identify the best alternative from those available, Kepner and Tregoe apply a set of weighted numerical scores to each. The weights reflect the relative importance of the various objectives satisfied by each alternative. The best alternative is the one with the highest numerical score. These scores, however, are simply numbers and bear no relation to the actual economic consequences that would result from selecting and implementing a specific alternative. In other words, the scores cannot be equated with any measure of gain or loss in evaluating the result of the decision.

Of all the problem-making methods discussed so far, the Kepner–Tregoe approach seems to have the greatest potential for helping managers improve their decision-making ability. However, even this procedure has deficiencies. Probably the most serious is that the problem of uncertainty is ignored. And uncertainty is the biggest obstacle to effective managerial decision making. It is all very well to evaluate alternatives in terms of their ability to satisfy objectives. However, it is extremely unlikely that any single alternative is always best, regardless of uncertain factors in the decision-making environment. On those rare occasions when this is the case, the manager is operating under conditions of certainty and decision making is relatively easy. The more common decision-making environment is one of uncertainty, and it is here that the manager is most in need of assistance.

In most decision situations the consequences of selecting any alternative are affected by uncertain conditions, or states of nature. The Kepner–Tregoe approach does not recognize these uncertainties except in the very final stage of evaluating the possible adverse consequences of a tentative decision. At that stage, a score is computed based in part on the likelihood that an adverse consequence will occur. However, even this comes too late in the decision-making procedure, and little is said about how these likelihoods are determined.

Despite these deficiencies, the Kepner–Tregoe approach, by systematizing and quantifying the decision process, does represent an improvement in managerial decision-making techniques. Unfortunately, it doesn't go far enough.

STATISTICAL DECISION THEORY

Statistical decision theory, or Bayesian decision theory, is a procedure for utilizing both numerical data and judgmental evaluations for making decisions under uncertainty that are optimal according to certain economic and statistical criteria. Theoretically, the method satisfies all the requirements of an effective managerial decision-making technique. It accommodates both empirical and judgmental data. It utilizes such data in a systematic and consistent manner in reaching an optimal decision. It specifies a logical economic criterion for determining the best alternative. And it provides a procedure for revising prior data and the decision resulting from them in the light of new or additional evidence. In these respects, it would seem to be an ideal decision-making tool. Unfortunately, it too has drawbacks.

The greatest difficulty encountered in applying this technique to managerial decision situations is that it requires an understanding of fairly complex mathematical and statistical models in all but the simplest types of decision situations. Most managers do not have the background in mathematics and statistics necessary to apply the procedure properly. Furthermore, most managers do not have either the time or the inclination to obtain this background. In addition, although the theory is beautifully simple in concept, its application to typically complex managerial decision situations can be extremely difficult, requiring the services of trained statisticians and computer programmers and the use of a large-scale digital computer. As a result, the technique is frequently uneconomical in light of the decisions to be made. In other words, it can cost more to use the technique than the optimal decision is worth.

Nevertheless, the basic concepts of statistical decision theory in the treatment of the problem of uncertainty and the development of criteria of optimality are too valuable to ignore. Many of the mathematical difficulties can be overcome through the use of approximations, shortcut techniques, and intuition. Many of the complexities can be simplified through common sense and judgment. In other words, it is possible to modify and simplify the theoretical decision-making model so that it can be used without resorting to difficult mathematics, specialists, or computers. It is the logic rather than the detail of the theory that is valuable. This simplified, logical, and intuitive version of statistical decision theory is what we refer to as formal intuitive decision making. The process is described in detail in the following chapters.

4

DESCRIBING THE DECISION SITUATION—THE PAYOFF TABLE

"If you can keep your head when all around you are losing theirs, you simply don't understand the problem."

At least 90% of the difficulties involved in problem solving can be eliminated by a complete, correct, clear, and concise statement of the problem. Let's refer to these characteristics of a problem statement as the four C's. The concept bears repeating: the problem description or statement must be *complete, correct, clear, and concise.*

In order for a problem description to be complete, all factors relating to the decision situation must be considered. Unimportant or inconsequential factors may be eliminated later, but they must not be ignored or forgotten in formulating the problem. A solution to an incomplete problem is bound to be an incomplete solution.

That the problem must be described correctly is obvious. Errors in problem formulation can lead only to incorrect solutions, and a correct solution to the wrong problem is just as bad as an incorrect solution to the right one. A clear and concise description is necessary for complete understanding by the decision maker. Consequently, the first and most important step in

37

the decision-making process is describing the decision situation.

In the real world, managerial decision situations can be very complex. For this reason, it is the rare decision maker who can construct and maintain a purely mental description of the decision situation, perform all the necessary evaluations, and make an optimal decision. For most managers, the descriptive and evaluation process is best accomplished with pencil and paper. An objective, written statement of the problem is the best way to ensure that it is described correctly and completely. A useful device for describing decision situations is discussed below.

PAYOFF TABLES

The general form of a payoff table was illustrated and described in Chapter 2. In a payoff table, all the available alternatives are listed across the top, either by a short description or by their symbols (a_1, a_2, a_3, and so on). The possible states of nature are listed in a column to the left of the table, again either by a short description or by their symbols (s_1, s_2, s_3, and so forth). The consequences, or more properly the conditional consequences, of each act for each state occupy the body of the table. In a payoff table describing a real decision situation, the consequences are numerical values. As mentioned previously, the consequences in most managerial decision situations are usually stated in monetary values. These monetary consequences may represent profit, cost, or loss.

The payoff table presents a picture of the decision situation at a single point in time. It displays all the factors that have a bearing on the decision in a clear and concise manner. Consequently, it is the best and most convenient description of what is called a *single-stage decision situation*—one that is resolved by a single decision made at one specific point in time. (We refer to the time at which a decision is made as the *decision date*.) There are, however, decision situations that cannot be resolved by a single decision. These situations require that a series of decisions be made over a period of time and are referred to as *multistage* or *sequential decision problems*. In a sequential decision situation, there is more than one decision date and each subsequent decision depends on a decision made previously. A multistage or sequential decision situation cannot be conveniently described with a payoff table and requires a device called a decision tree. We will discuss decision trees later.

A payoff table provides a complete, correct, clear, and concise description of a single-stage decision situation for the decision maker. With the payoff table, the decision maker has all the factors relating to the problem and their relationships at his fingertips. Another major benefit of the table is that in the process of constructing it, the decision maker must become thoroughly familiar with all aspects of the decision situation. First he must identify and list all the alternatives available to him. He must screen his initial list of alternatives, retaining only those that are real and viable and eliminating those that are not. The final set of alternatives must be all-inclusive and mutually exclusive. All-inclusive means that every available viable alternative is included. Mutually exclusive means that each alternative is a distinct and separate act and is not included in any other alternative.

For example, in analyzing a lease-or-buy decision situation, the decision maker might initially list these alternatives:

a_1: lease
a_2: don't lease
a_3: buy

However, a little additional thought reveals that a_2 and a_3 are not mutually exclusive. The alternative "don't lease" includes the alternative "buy." If the decision maker wants to consider the situation as a two-action problem in which the alternative "don't lease" includes all possible alternatives to "lease," then he should list the alternatives for this situation as follows:

a_1: lease
a_2: don't lease

Acts a_1 and a_2 are now mutually exclusive. On the other hand, if the decision maker sees his alternatives as being "lease," "buy," or "do neither," the mutually exclusive alternatives should be listed as follows:

a_1: lease

a_2: buy

a_3: neither lease nor buy

Once the possible alternatives have been listed, the decision maker must identify and list all the uncontrollable factors or states of nature that could affect the consequences of each act. The list of states should also be all-inclusive and mutually exclusive. Finally, every·act must be evaluated against every state to determine the conditional consequences. In the course of preparing the payoff table, the decision maker becomes thoroughly familiar with every aspect of the situation and consequently is not likely to overlook any important factor. The process itself can be as valuable to the decision maker as the end result, the payoff table.

Consider a simple example. Electronic Devices, Inc. specializes in the development and manufacture of electronic and electro-mechanical components used in many different types of systems. EDI recently received a request for proposal from a government agency for the development and manufacture of a substantial quantity of an electronic component that must meet a set of rigid specifications. The engineering vice president of EDI has no doubt about the ability of his organization to develop the component, but the cost of preparing the proposal is estimated to be $95,000, since several design approaches must be investigated. However, if EDI is awarded the contract, it is estimated that the company will profit by $350,000.

To be more precise, the $350,000 represents *contribution* to profit and is defined as the net cash inflow less the net cash outflow associated with the alternative. Contribution in dollars is the most common evaluation unit for business decision situations. Of course, when cash outflow exceeds cash inflow for a particular alternative, the contribution is negative and represents a loss.

The calculation or estimate of the contribution associated with a specific alternative for a given state of nature should be based on accounting information, engineering estimates, cost estimates, and other hard data when available. The $350,000 contribution to profit, which represents the consequence of the act "submit bid" *if* EDI is awarded the contract, results from the collection and analysis of data submitted to the decision maker by subordinates. It is not likely that the decision maker himself would gather and analyze the data. The formal intuitive decision procedure indicates how these data should be used, but not necessarily how they are obtained. More about this later.

There are only two alternatives to be considered in this decision problem:

a_1:   bid
a_2:   decline to bid

When only two alternatives are considered, the decision situation is referred to as a two-action problem. The states of nature—that is, the uncontrollable factors that will affect the consequences of EDI's decision—are the uncertain actions of the potential customer, the government agency. So, as far as EDI is concerned, the possible states are:

s_1:   EDI gets contract
s_2:   EDI doesn't get contract

Notice that the decision situation is exactly reversed from the customer's point of view. The alternatives in the customer's decision situation are "award contract to EDI" and "don't award contract to EDI"—the states of nature in EDI's decision situation.

Once alternatives and states have been identified, the next step is to associate a conditional consequence with each act for every state of nature and to arrange the information into a table. The conditional consequences can be obtained from the statement of the problem. If a_1 is chosen, the consequence depends on whether EDI is awarded the contract. If s_1 occurs with a_1, the payoff is $350,000. If s_2 occurs with a_1, the payoff is a negative contribution or loss of $95,000, which will be shown as −$95,000. If EDI chooses a_2 (declines to bid), the consequences will be the same for both possible states, a contribution of $0. In other words, if EDI declines to bid there is no cash outflow and no cash inflow. The payoff table for this decision is illustrated in Figure 4.1.

The payoff table by itself is not a solution to a decision problem. The table simply displays all the factors in the problem—the alternatives, the states, and the conditional consequences—in a manner that makes it easy for the decision maker to comprehend the situation. Whether an action that can lead to a $350,000 profit or a $95,000 loss with some degree of uncertainty is preferable to another action with a certain outcome of $0 profit or loss cannot be determined without dealing with the uncertainties of the states in some way. In order to do this, we must first establish some criterion for dealing with these uncertainties and making a decision. Various decision criteria will be discussed later.

Once the payoff table is constructed, the decision maker can use it to review the problem and determine if the description of the situation is indeed complete and correct. Suppose that the executive vice president of EDI, who has final responsibility for the bid decision, realizes that the payoff table in Figure 4.1 is neither complete nor correct for this decision situation. The alternatives available to EDI are not limited to "bid" or "no bid"—EDI could make bids at different levels. In fact, the cost analysts who provided the vice president with data included three different prices at which the bid could be submitted. These will be referred to as a high price, a moderate price, and a low price. The analysts suggest that the lower the bid, the greater the likelihood that EDI would win the award.

Of course, the lower the bid price, the smaller the contribution to profit if EDI does get the contract. The data indicate that if EDI were to bid high, and get the contract, the contribution to profit would be $475,000. The moderate bid would produce a contribution to profit of $350,000, while the low bid would

FIGURE 4.1 Payoff table for simple EDI bid decision.

STATES	ACTS	
	a_1: bid	a_2: decline to bid
s_1: EDI gets contract	$350,000	$0
s_2: EDI doesn't get contract	−$ 95,000	$0

produce a contribution of $125,000. Consequently, the more realistic situation requires a choice among four, not two, alternatives:

a_1: bid high
a_2: bid moderate
a_3: bid low
a_4: no bid

In some decision situations, the states of nature that must be considered may be independent of the choices available to the decision maker. When it is reasonable to assume that such independence exists, expanding the set of alternatives as we have just done would not automatically require an expanded set of states. For the four alternatives listed above the states could still be:

s_1: EDI gets contract
s_2: EDI doesn't get contract

The payoff table for this situation is shown in Figure 4.2.

SIMPLIFYING THE DECISION PROBLEM

In addition to being complete and correct, the description of a decision situation should be as simple as possible. One way to simplify a decision problem is to eliminate from the set of alternatives any act that is inferior to some other act. The payoff table makes it easy for the decision maker to determine which acts dominate others. A *dominant act* is one for which the conditional consequences are as good as or better than those of another act for all states of nature and distinctly better than those of the other act for at least one state. The act or acts that are

FIGURE 4.2   Initial payoff table for modified EDI bid decision.

STATES	ACTS			
	a_1: high bid	a_2: moderate bid	a_3: low bid	a_4: no bid
s_1: EDI gets contract	$475,000	$350,000	$125,000	$0
s_2: EDI doesn't get contract	−$ 95,000	−$ 95,000	−$ 95,000	$0

dominated are *inferior acts* and can be eliminated from consideration.

Look again at Figure 4.2. Compare the conditional consequences of a_2 and a_3 with a_1. Notice that for s_2, the consequences of these three acts are identical. However, for s_1, the payoff associated with a_1 is higher than for the other two. Act a_1 is as good as the others for s_2 and distinctly better for s_1. Therefore a_1 dominates a_2 and a_3, which are inferior.

Now compare a_1 and a_4. The payoff of a_1 is higher than that of a_4 if s_1 is the state of nature—\$475,000 is certainly greater than \$0. However, the payoff of a_4 is greater than that of a_1 if s_2 is the state of nature, since \$0 is greater than $-\$95,000$. Consequently, neither of these acts dominates the other and neither is an inferior act.

Assuming that the states in this situation are independent of the alternatives—that is, that the price bid has no effect on whether EDI is awarded the contract—then acts a_2 and a_3 should not even be considered. EDI should either bid high or not at all. Consequently, the payoff table for this problem should appear as shown in Figure 4.3, with acts a_2 and a_3 eliminated.

Unfortunately, the assumption that the acts and states in this problem are independent is obviously false. The price bid by EDI will certainly have an effect on its chances of getting the contract. Whatever that effect is (a point we will consider later), the fact that it exists requires that we reassess the number of states to be considered in the problem. If the level of the bid affects the likelihood that EDI will be awarded the contract, we must consider a separate state for each level at which EDI might submit a bid. The new set of states for this problem might be:

s_1: EDI gets contract with high bid
s_2: EDI gets contract with moderate bid
s_3: EDI gets contract with low bid
s_4: EDI doesn't get contract

Is this an accurate representation of the states bearing on the decision? Not quite. At least, not without some explanation. What happens if EDI submits a moderate or low bid and s_1 occurs? Does s_1 imply that EDI would get the contract if it bid high but not if the company bid moderate or low? It seems

FIGURE 4.3 Reduced payoff table
for modified EDI bid decision.

STATES	ACTS	
	a_1: high bid	a_2: no bid
s_1: EDI gets contract	$475,000	$0
s_2: EDI doesn't get contract	−$ 95,000	$0

obvious that if EDI prepares a proposal good enough to get the contract with a high bid, it would also get the contract with a low or moderate bid. Under s_2, if EDI would be awarded the contract with a moderate bid, it would also get the contract with a low bid but not with a high bid. Finally, under s_3, EDI would be awarded the contract with a low bid but not with a moderate or high bid. The states are probably better expressed as follows:

s_1: EDI gets contract with high, moderate, or low bid
s_2: EDI gets contract with moderate or low bid
s_3: EDI gets contract with low bid
s_4: EDI doesn't get contract

The complete and accurate representation of the decision situation is provided in Figure 4.4.

Whenever a payoff table is revised, the decision maker should make a final check for completeness and accuracy. This includes a check for inferior acts and for inconsequential states. We have already discussed inferior acts, and a check of Figure 4.4 shows that none of the alternatives listed is inferior. An inconsequential state is one that has exactly the same consequences for all the alternatives as some other state. When this occurs, the states with

FIGURE 4.4 Final payoff table for modified EDI bid decision.

STATES	ACTS			
	a_1	a_2	a_3	a_4
s_1	$475,000	$350,000	$125,000	$0
s_2	−$ 95,000	$350,000	$125,000	$0
s_3	−$ 95,000	−$ 95,000	$125,000	$0
s_4	−$ 95,000	−$ 95,000	−$ 95,000	$0

identical consequences can be combined and considered as a single state of nature. Inspection indicates that none of the states in Figure 4.4 is inconsequential.

A DECISION-MAKING DIALOGUE

It might not be immediately obvious how the decision maker progressed from the statement of the problem as illustrated by the two-action and two-state payoff table in Figure 4.1 to the final payoff table in Figure 4.4. To show how this process might have occurred, let's reconstruct a hypothetical conversation between the decision maker and the staff assistant who submitted the preliminary payoff table as a first try at describing the decision problem.

ASST: Do you think that this is a complete and correct description of the problem?

  DM: Well, I suppose it's correct as far as it goes, but after looking at the table, I really don't think it presents a complete picture of the situation.

ASST: What do you think is missing?

  DM: For one thing, we really have more alternatives than bid or not bid. From the information I have, we could consider three different prices for our proposal. The $350,-000 payoff shown on the table as the consequence of bidding and getting the contract would result from bidding at the intermediate or moderate price. Our cost analysts have also come up with a higher price and a lower price.

ASST: Yes, that's right. According to the analysis, if we bid high and get the contract our profit would be $475,000 and if we bid low and win our profit would be $125,000. However, in setting up the payoff table, I thought that the moderate price would be the most reasonable, so that's the one I used.

  DM: It seems to me that since these various prices are options available to us, they should be included as alternatives in the decision situation and shown on the table. Eliminating two of those options is itself a decision that should undergo the same analysis as any other decision. We really have four alternatives here: bid high, bid moderate, bid low, and decline to bid. Let's rework the table to reflect all the options.

At this point, the staff assistant makes the necessary changes in the payoff table and comes up with the table illustrated in Figure 4.2. The decision maker studies the new table and the conversation continues:

DM: A payoff table certainly does clarify the situation. One fact is apparent which didn't occur to me before. If this table is complete and correct as it stands, it would not pay even to consider making the low or moderate bid. If we get the contract, we are obviously much better off with the high bid; and if we don't get the contract, we are no worse off. If this is correct, we should either bid high or decline to bid. The other two alternatives are clearly inferior.

ASST: That appears to be true, but maybe we are still overlooking something.

DM: Yes, what we appear to be overlooking, or possibly over-simplifying, are the states. These two states might be appropriate for the simple "bid" or "no bid" decision that we started with, but with the new, expanded set of alternatives they don't seem to be adequate.

ASST: In what way aren't they adequate?

DM: Let me answer that question with another question. What effect do you think our price would have on our chances of getting the contract?

ASST: Well, I suppose that, everything else being equal, the higher we bid the less chance we have of getting the contract.

DM: Right. And if that is true, then we have to consider a separate state to coincide with each level at which we might price the proposal.

ASST: In other words the states for this problem should be:

s_1: EDI gets contract with high bid
s_2: EDI gets contract with moderate bid
s_3: EDI gets contract with low bid
s_4: EDI doesn't get contract

DM: Wait a minute. Let's not jump to conclusions. We had better analyze the implications of each one of these states in the context of our decision situation. What does s_1 actually mean the way we have stated it? Does it imply that we get the contract with the high bid but not with a lower bid? That doesn't make sense. I think it is obvious that if our proposal is good enough to get us the contract at a high price, it is good enough to get us the contract at a lower price. I believe that a more accurate way to define the states is:

s_1: EDI gets contract with high, moderate, or low bid
s_2: EDI gets contract with moderate or low bid
s_3: EDI gets contract with low bid
s_4: EDI doesn't get contract

Give it another try and let me see a payoff table that reflects the four alternatives and the four appropriate states.

The staff assistant now prepares the table illustrated in Figure 4.4. This is a complete and correct representation of the problem. As in most complex decision situations, the final payoff table is a result of several attempts and successive approximations.

It is important that the payoff table be as complete and accurate as possible. Of course, completeness and accuracy depend on the amount and accuracy of information available to the decision maker. Completeness and accuracy also depend on the amount of time the decision maker has to make a decision. The more time he has, the more information he can acquire. When important information is not available and there is insufficient time to acquire it, the decision maker must use his judgment in making estimates and assessments. The judgment of the decision maker is paramount throughout the process.

Notice that in the final payoff table for the EDI bid decision (Figure 4.4) there is no single act that provides the highest payoff for all the states of nature. If there were, we would have a single dominant act and the decision would be simple. Furthermore, if we were certain as to which state of nature would occur, the decision problem would also be simple. We would merely select that alternative with the highest payoff under the certain state of nature. But, of course, that would be decision making under certainty.

When uncertainty exists, as it does in almost all managerial decision situations, there is always some chance that the decision maker will make a wrong or less than optimal decision. It is important to remember that under uncertainty there is no procedure that will *always* lead to the right decision. But by dealing with uncertainty in a logical and consistent manner, the decision maker can achieve a significant preponderance of good decisions over poor ones.

At this stage we have not yet considered how to deal with the uncertainty in the decision situation. We have been concerned only with describing the situation in a clear and concise manner using the payoff table. The steps required for constructing a payoff table are summarized as follows:

1. Check to be sure that the situation requires that only one decision be made at a single point in time. In other words, be sure that the decision situation does not involve a sequence of decisions over an extended period of time.
2. Specify a cutoff or *evaluation date* for the decision. This is the date at which all the major consequences of the decision can be evaluated.
3. List all the alternatives available to the decision maker in the decision situation.
4. Specify all the states of nature (uncontrollable factors) that will have an effect on the consequence of any alternative.
5. Begin constructing the table by assigning and labeling a column for each alternative and a row for each possible state.
6. For each alternative, determine the numerical value of the payoff or consequence given each possible state. Place that value at the intersection of the appropriate row and column.
7. Check for and eliminate inferior alternatives.
8. Check for and eliminate inconsequential states.

COMPLEXITY VERSUS COMPLETENESS

Completeness is of paramount importance in describing a decision situation. Unless the situation is completely described, we are likely to overlook some factor that has or could have some significant effect on the consequences of the decision. However, in striving for completeness, we may make the decision problem so complicated that it defies solution.

In any decision situation, particularly in practical managerial decision situations, it is possible to think of an almost unlimited number of factors that might have some effect on the results of the decision. The number is almost unlimited, that is, if we consider any effect no matter how small and every factor regardless of how remote its possibility. It is also possible to enumerate an enormous number of possible alternatives, if no regard is given to their practicality.

Consequently, common sense dictates that the decision maker exercise judgment in simplifying the decision problem as much as possible. We have already provided two rules for simplifying: eliminating inferior acts and eliminating inconsequential states. In addition, since the decision maker has control over the alternatives to be considered in the decision situation, he should use informed judgment in determining initially which alternatives should be used in the formal decision-making procedure. Furthermore, even though the decision maker has no control over the states of nature—he can't make an unwanted state go away by ignoring it—he should be able to eliminate the extremely unlikely and/or unimportant factors without formal analysis.

Remember that the final description of the decision situation results from a series of successive approximations. Each successive revision can either add or eliminate alternatives and states as necessary. The end result of the process should be a model of the decision situation that is correct and comprehensible to the decision maker and facilitates the decision-making process. If the tool used leads to confusion rather than enlightenment, its purpose is defeated.

Practice is essential to the master of any technique. Managers, by virtue of their position and responsibilities, get plenty of practice in decision making. However, there is usually a significant lag between the making of a decision and the time at which its correctness or optimality can be determined. Furthermore, on-the-job decision making cannot be done in simple stages, with a check for correctness after each stage. It is pretty much an all-or-nothing proposition. Several additional decision situations are described below to give the reader practice in preparing payoff tables. The correct solutions are provided at the end of each example.

In studying these and all the other examples that appear in this book, keep in mind that they represent a compromise between realism and simplicity. If an example is overly complex, the principle to be illustrated may be lost in the intricacies of the problem. On the other hand, if the example is oversimplified, it may bear little relation to the real-world problems with which the manager must contend. Generally the first examples in any set are the simplest. We will frequently return to the same examples throughout the book but add further complexities as new topics are covered.

The Granger Case

Paul Granger owns 25 acres of land on the route of a proposed expressway. If the route is approved, he will be paid $750,000 for the land by the state highway department. If the route is not approved, he intends to subdivide the land into one-acre lots and sell them individually. Granger estimates that he could sell each lot for $22,500. However, he would incur subdividing and sales costs of $3,500 per lot.

Granger has just received an offer of $600,000 for the land from the Southeastern Mutual Life Insurance Company, which plans to use it for the construction of a new home-office building. Granger must accept or reject the offer within 72 hours. Describe this decision situation using a payoff table.

Alternatives

a_1: accept offer (of insurance company)
a_2: reject offer

States

s_1:   expressway route is approved

s_2:   expressway route is not approved

Consequences

If Granger accepts the offer made by Southeastern Mutual, he will receive $600,000, and the payoff for this act will be the same regardless of whether the expressway route is approved. If he rejects the offer, he could receive $750,000 if the route is approved or $475,000 if the route is not approved. The $475,000 would result from the sale of 25 building lots at $22,500 − $3,500 = $19,000 each.

Decision date and evaluation date

The decision date for this problem is 72 hours from the receipt of the offer from the insurance company. The evaluation date is the date at which all consequences can be evaluated. The decision of the state highway department is expected to be known in 60 days. However, the lot sales, if the property is subdivided and sold as individual lots, would be completed in one year. Consequently, the cutoff date for evaluating the consequences is one year from the decision date.

This brings up the question of the present value of a cash payment received some time in the future. In other words, in evaluating the consequences, we are comparing the value of an immediate payment from the insurance company with a future payment either from the state or from individual buyers of the building lots. We could discount the future payment and compute its *present value* by a simple formula common in financial analysis. In this instance, however, it is unlikely that using the discounted value of the future payment instead of the actual value would have any effect on the decision. Consequently, we will use the actual value here. However it is up to the decision maker to estimate or evaluate the payoffs to the best of his ability in any decision situation. In some cases, this might require that he use a discounted value.

Payoff table

The payoff table should appear as shown in Figure 4.5.

FIGURE 4.5   Payoff table for Granger
land decision.

STATES	ACTS	
	a_1	a_2
s_1	$600,000	$750,000
s_2	$600,000	$475,000

The Thompson Case

Frank Thompson is the sole proprietor of Frank Thompson &
Associates, General Contractors. Thompson recently received a
letter from the president of Tristate Development Company, a
developer of exclusive residential communities. Tristate recently
acquired a 100-acre tract of land in Thompson's general area,
which is zoned for single-family residences on minimum two-acre
lots. Tristate plans to subdivide this acreage into 50 lots, put in
streets, sewers, and utilities, and sell the lots to selected builders.
The builders invited to participate were chosen because of their
reputation for high-quality construction and their experience in
building houses in the appropriate price range. The houses
constructed on the lots must be custom-built and must sell in the
range of $90,000 to $125,000. Thompson is offered up to five
lots at $16,000 per lot.

Frank Thompson's decision to purchase one, two, three, four,
or five lots or none at all will depend on his potential payoff
from these alternatives. He has plans for a house that can be
priced to sell for $95,000. Since he has already built several
houses from these plans, he is able to estimate his construction
costs quite accurately at $60,000. His selling costs, commissions,
and advertising average about $2,000 per house. These costs,
plus the cost of the lot, add up to $78,000, providing him with a
profit of $17,000 on each house he can sell.

The uncertain events, or states of nature, in this case relate to
the demand for houses in the appropriate price range in the
area. In order for the investment to be profitable, Thompson
feels that he must be able to get his money out within one year.
In other words, the cutoff date for the evaluation of the decision
is one year from the decision date. Describe the decision situation using a payoff table.

Alternatives

Thompson has six alternatives. He can purchase anywhere from zero to five lots. We will designate these alternatives as a_0 through a_5, as follows:

a_0: purchase no lots
a_1: purchase one lot
a_2: purchase two lots
a_3: purchase three lots
a_4: purchase four lots
a_5: purchase five lots

States

The consequences of this decision are affected by the local demand for housing. However, Thompson cannot and should not attempt to determine the overall demand for houses of this type in his area. His concern is with his ability to sell the house or houses he builds within one year. Of course, the demand for his houses will depend to some extent on the overall demand. It will also depend on the quality of his houses and his marketing ability. Consequently, the states in this problem are the levels of demand for Thompson's houses should he decide to build:

s_0: demand for no houses
s_1: demand for one house
s_2: demand for two houses
s_3: demand for three houses
s_4: demand for four houses
s_5: demand for five houses

Consequences

The consequence for each alternative and state can be determined directly from the statement of the decision situation. If Thompson turns down the offer—that is, selects alternative a_0—his payoff for all states is simply \$0. For all the other alternatives, the payoff is equal to the cash inflow less the cash outflow. The cash outflow is \$78,000 times the number of houses he builds. The cash inflow is \$95,000 times the number of houses he is able to sell. The payoff table is shown in Figure 4.6.

To illustrate the computation of the payoffs, let's run through a few of the calculations. Suppose that Thompson se-

FIGURE 4.6   Payoff table for Frank Thompson & Associates.

STATES	ACTS					
	a_0	a_1	a_2	a_3	a_4	a_5
s_0	$0	−$78,000	−$156,000	−$234,000	−$312,000	−$390,000
s_1	$0	$17,000	−$ 61,000	−$139,000	−$217,000	−$295,000
s_2	$0	$17,000	$ 34,000	−$ 44,000	−$122,000	−$200,000
s_3	$0	$17,000	$ 34,000	$ 51,000	−$ 27,000	−$105,000
s_4	$0	$17,000	$ 34,000	$ 51,000	$ 68,000	−$ 10,000
s_5	$0	$17,000	$ 34,000	$ 51,000	$ 68,000	$ 85,000

lects a_2 and builds two houses. His total investment is 2 × $78,000 = $156,000. If he sells neither house—that is, state s_0— his payoff is −$156,000, or a loss of $156,000. If he sells just one house, his cash inflow is $95,000. However, since he has paid out $156,000, his payoff is $95,000 − $156,000 = −$61,000. If he sells both houses, he receives 2 × $95,000 = $190,000. This less his investment of $156,000 leaves him with a profit of $34,000. The $34,000 payoff is also twice the profit of $17,000 per house. If there is a demand for three or more houses—that is, s_3 through s_5—Thompson's profit will still be only $34,000, since he can't sell more houses than he has built. The same reasoning applies to the payoffs in all the other columns.

Examination of the table shows that there are no dominant or inferior acts and no inconsequential states.

The Eastways Case

Eastways Sales Corporation, a manufacturer's representative, has been offered a new product line by one of its manufacturers. The new line can be handled in one of two ways. The better way, according to the manufacturer, is for Eastways to establish a separate division to handle the new line exclusively. This would require a separate sales office, staff, and sales force plus an initial investment of $250,000 for the office, equipment, and the hiring and training of personnel. If the new line could be handled by the existing organization, the initial investment would only be $50,000, principally for the training of the present sales staff.

The average price of a product in the new line is $350. Eastways normally receives 20% of the sales price for each unit sold, of which 10% is paid as commission to the salesperson. In order to encourage Eastways to establish the separate sales division, the manufacturer offers to pay 30% for each unit sold. If Eastways does not set up the new division, the normal 20% will be paid.

The cutoff date for evaluating the decision is one year from the decision date. Eastways estimates that sales of the new product could range from 2,000 to 8,000 units during the first year. Describe this decision situation using a payoff table.

Alternatives

There are three alternatives available to Eastways:

a_1: accept new line and establish separate division
a_2: accept new line and use existing organization
a_3: reject new line

States

The factors affecting the consequences of the alternatives are related to sales of the new product during the period up to the evaluation date. According to Eastways' estimate, sales could range from as few as 2,000 units to as many as 8,000 units during this period. Since each unit sold makes some difference in the payoff, we could conceivably identify a separate state for each sale of one additional unit—that is, s_1: 2,000 units sold; s_2: 2,001 units sold; s_3: 2,002 units sold; and so on. However, this would result in about 6,000 different states of nature, many of which would be inconsequential. Such a situation would be impossible to describe with a payoff table.

Since a one-unit change in sales is unlikely to have any significant effect on the consequences, it seems reasonable to differentiate among the states by some larger figure. For example, we might define the states in terms of differentials of 1,000 units. This would certainly reduce the number of states to be contended with and create a clear and concise description of the situation. If, as the analysis proceeds, it appears that these increments are too large, we can always revise the description by using smaller units. As a start, then, we will define the states as:

s_1: 2,000 units sold
s_2: 3,000 units sold
s_3: 4,000 units sold
s_4: 5,000 units sold
s_5: 6,000 units sold
s_6: 7,000 units sold
s_7: 8,000 units sold

Consequences

The payoffs are the difference between net cash inflow and net cash outflow resulting from an alternative and a specific state. For a_1, the cash outflow is the initial required investment of $250,000. The cash inflow is 20% (30% less the salesperson's commission of 10%) of the number of units sold times $350. For a_2, the cash outflow is $50,000. The cash inflow is 10% (20% less the salesperson's commission of 10%) of the number of units sold times $350. For a_3, the payoff is $0 for all states. The first approximation to the payoff table is given in Figure 4.7.

The payoff table must be examined for dominant and inferior acts and inconsequential states. It is apparent that a_1 is better than a_2 for some states and worse for others. Consequently, neither a_1 nor a_2 dominates the other. However, a_3 is definitely inferior to a_2 for all the states. Therefore, a_3 is dominated by a_2 and should be eliminated from consideration. None of the states is inconsequential. The revised payoff table is shown in Figure 4.8.

FIGURE 4.7   Initial Eastways payoff table.

STATES	ACTS		
	a_1	a_2	a_3
s_1	−$110,000	$ 20,000	$0
s_2	−$ 40,000	$ 55,000	$0
s_3	$ 30,000	$ 90,000	$0
s_4	$100,000	$125,000	$0
s_5	$170,000	$160,000	$0
s_6	$240,000	$195,000	$0
s_7	$300,000	$230,000	$0

FIGURE 4.8   Final Eastways payoff table.

STATES	ACTS	
	a_1	a_2
s_1	−$110,000	$ 20,000
s_2	−$ 40,000	$ 55,000
s_3	$ 30,000	$ 90,000
s_4	$100,000	$125,000
s_5	$170,000	$160,000
s_6	$240,000	$195,000
s_7	$300,000	$230,000

The Thermocal Case

Thermocal, Inc. is a medium-size company that has manufactured and marketed heating and air-conditioning equipment and systems for over 30 years. Its products include room and central air conditioning units, heating systems, and heat pumps. Sales are made directly to builders and contractors and through retail stores. Thermocal has an excellent reputation for quality and reliability. However, in the past few years sales have leveled off because of increased competition, a decrease in housing starts, and a general decline in demand resulting from various economic factors, not the least of which are inflation and increasing energy costs. As a result, profits have declined and Thermocal has failed to pay a quarterly dividend for the first time in 27 years.

Thermocal holds a yearly planning meeting in July which brings the top executives of the company together for a week. This year's meeting is especially important, because top management must make plans and decisions that affect the future of the company. Various proposals have been made as to the actions and direction Thermocal should take in order to overcome its present difficulties. One promising idea is to capitalize on the energy situation and make a substantial investment in developing a solar power system for residential use. Researchers in the engineering division have prepared a proposal for a system of solar panels which operate in conjunction with a new superefficient heat pump to provide a complete residential heating and cooling system partially based on solar energy. The system is designed to be installed during the construction of new houses or to replace present systems in existing structures.

The engineering feasibility of the system has been established. However, considerable development is still required before the system can be manufactured and marketed. The cost of development is estimated to be $2.5 million and will result in a prototype model that can be put into production. It is estimated that the prototype can be developed in 18 months and that the first commercial system can be delivered in 2½ years. If a decision is made to proceed with the development, an additional

$500,000 will have to be spent on advertising and promotion, bringing the total investment in the project to $3 million. The engineers estimate that if Thermocal goes into production, it could manufacture up to 10,000 systems per year with its present production facilities.

Many uncertainties exist regarding the potential success of this project. The first involves the size of the market for a solar power system of this type two to three years in the future. A major factor affecting market size is the price at which the system will be sold. The price in turn depends on manufacturing costs, which include material and labor costs 18 months in the future. These costs are unknown and can only be estimated at this time. Another key factor is the general state of the economy at the time the new system is marketed, since economic conditions will affect the demand for housing. Still another uncertainty involves possible competition. Thermocal believes that it is well ahead of any potential competitor in the development of a system of this type. However, it would be unrealistic to assume that no other companies are looking into similar approaches to the energy situation. The longer it takes Thermocal to reach the market with its system, the more likely it is that competition will develop.

An alternative to the solar power project has been presented to the executives by the marketing vice president. He proposes that an extensive advertising and promotional campaign be launched to improve the sales of Thermocal's present products and overcome the inroads that competitors have made into Thermocal's markets. The campaign would include extensive television advertising, partial sponsorship of a television series, and institutional advertising in various publications. The program would cost an estimated $1 million per year for two years and, according to the marketing VP, should result in a larger share of the market, increased sales, and higher profits. Of course, these results are also uncertain.

Finally, it is evident that a third alternative exists: simply do nothing and hope to ride out the hard times. This view is espoused by several members of the executive committee, who remind the group that the company has encountered difficulties before and survived. Their rationale is that economic conditions will improve and doing nothing requires no large capital investment.

The president and chief executive officer of Thermocal must make a decision and take his recommendations to the board of directors, which meets on August 15. Although any decision of this magnitude must be approved by the board, the president's recommendations are usually followed. As usual, the buck stops with the president and he will eventually be held responsible for the consequences of whatever decision he makes. The president is faced with a complex decision situation involving millions of dollars and the future of his company, and he must decide quickly and efficiently under conditions of uncertainty.

No managerial decision, particularly one as complicated as this, can be made in a vacuum. The decision maker—in this case, the president of Thermocal—must have some information on which to base his judgment. The formal intuitive approach requires informed judgment, not guesses. Estimates of sales and costs must be available in order for the payoffs to be computed. The payoffs for this problem will be additional contributions to profit under each alternative and every state. We will assume a decision date of August 15, 1981 and an evaluation date at the end of the first full fiscal year following the introduction of the new solar power system—that is, December 31, 1984.

Alternatives

The alternatives in this situation are:

a_1: develop and market the solar power system
a_2: implement the new advertising program
a_3: maintain the status quo

States

Defining the states of nature in this situation is quite complicated. Payoffs for a_1 will depend on future sales of the new system, which will in turn depend on several other uncertain events. First, sales of the system will be influenced to some extent by its eventual price, which in turn is a function of future costs. Sales will also be affected by the general condition of the economy, of which the major determining factor is the inflation rate.

Finally, sales will be affected by the presence or absence of competition.

Attempting to account for every element of each of these factors would be futile. In order to describe the decision situation so that it can be comprehended and analyzed, we must reduce the total number of possible states to a few broad categories for which estimates can be made. For example, the first two factors, price and general economic conditions, are related. The greater the rate of inflation, the higher the costs of labor and materials and consequently the higher the selling price of the system. In order to keep the number of states at a minimum, we can let general economic conditions summarize all the factors involved in demand and price.

The number of possible states of the economy is a matter of subjective judgment, but again in the interest of simplicity let's consider, at least initially, three economic states: good, fair, and poor. We can define these states by relating them to some economic measure, such as the rate of inflation or unemployment. Our definitions may be arbitrary, but some yardstick must be adopted, and we assume that the criteria adopted by the president of Thermocal is based on informed judgment and an assessment of the effects of these conditions on the market.

Another factor that will affect sales of the solar energy system is competition. If there is no competition at the time the system is introduced, Thermocal will have the entire market to itself. If one or more competitive systems are on the market, Thermocal's market share will be reduced. Since the number and status of potential competitors is unknown at this time, Thermocal can only assume the possible states of "competition" and "no competition."

We now have two categories of states: those having to do with the economy and those having to do with competition. The economy is considered to have three states and the competition two. Considering all combinations of states of the economy and states of the competition, we arrive at six initial states for the decision situation. These are:

s_1: economy good and no competition
s_2: economy good and competition
s_3: economy fair and no competition

s_4:   economy fair and competition
s_5:   economy poor and no competition
s_6:   economy poor and competition

Consequences

The payoff of each alternative for every state must now be estimated. Consider first a_1 (develop and market the solar power system). Market estimates under each possible state and payoffs based on these estimates are summarized in Tables 4.1 and 4.2. Notice that in Table 4.1 Thermocal's market share with competition is assumed to be 50%. This is the best estimate that can be made at this time, since no information is available about potential competitors. However, since Thermocal's production capacity is only 10,000 systems, under good economic conditions competition will have no effect on its sales.

The estimates of contribution in Table 4.2 are based on the following considerations. Thermocal's costs will increase and profits decrease as the state of the economy changes from good to fair to poor. If the economy is good, each unit sold will contribute \$1,400 to profit. With the economy fair, this contribution decreases to \$1,000, and with the economy poor it is only \$800. The contribution figures shown in the table result from multiplying the estimated unit sales by the per-unit contribution and subtracting the \$3 million investment required.

Similar payoff estimates must be made for the other alternatives. For a_2 (new advertising campaign), the payoffs are affected by the economy but not by the presence or absence of competition in the solar energy field. Therefore, for states s_1 and s_2 (economy good), it is estimated that profits over the period of the new campaign will increase by \$8 million, after deducting the

TABLE 4.1   Estimates of solar power system sales (in units).

State	No Competition		Competition	
	Total Market	Thermocal Share	Total Market	Thermocal Share
Economy good	20,000	10,000 (capacity)	20,000	10,000 (capacity)
Economy fair	12,000	10,000 (capacity)	12,000	6,000
Economy poor	3,750	3,750	3,750	1,875

TABLE 4.2   Estimated profit contribution from
solar power system sales.

State	No Competition	Competition
Economy good	$11 million	$11 million
Economy fair	$ 7 million	$ 3 million
Economy poor	$ 0	−$ 1.5 million

cost of the advertising campaign. Under states s_3 and s_4 (economy fair), the estimate is a net increase of $4 million; and under states s_5 and s_6 (economy poor), the estimate is a net increase of $2 million.

For a_3 (status quo), the payoffs are again affected only by the state of the economy. If the economy improves (economy good), it is estimated that profits will increase by $4 million. If the economy does not change (economy fair), it is estimated that there will be no change in profits. If economic conditions get worse (economy poor), there will be a decline in profits of $4 million. The first approximation to the payoff table for the Thermocal decision situation is provided in Figure 4.9.

Examining the figure for inferior acts and inconsequential states, we can see that a_3 is inferior to both a_1 and a_2 for all the states and should be eliminated. Also, states s_1 and s_2 have identical consequences for all the alternatives. This is because under good economic conditions sales are limited by production capacity and are not affected by the presence or absence of competition. Competition is inconsequential under these conditions and should be eliminated. As a result, s_1 and s_2 become a single state

FIGURE 4.9   First approximation to payoff table
for Thermocal.

STATES	ACTS		
	a_1	a_2	a_3
s_1	$11 million	$8 million	$4 million
s_2	$11 million	$8 million	$4 million
s_3	$ 7 million	$4 million	$ 0
s_4	$ 3.5 million	$4 million	$ 0
s_5	$ 0	$2 million	−$4 million
s_6	−$ 1.5 million	$2 million	−$4 million

labeled "economy good," and the remaining states can be renumbered as follows:

s_1: economy good

s_2: economy fair and no competition

s_3: economy fair and competition

s_4: economy poor and no competition

s_5: economy poor and competition

The revised payoff table is shown in Figure 4.10.

The examples above are exercises in describing single-stage decision situations using payoff tables. This is only the first stage in the decision process. The problem of making optimal choices from the available alternatives will be examined in the coming chapters.

FIGURE 4.10   Final payoff table for Thermocal decision.

STATES	ACTS	
	a_1	a_2
s_1	$11 million	$8 million
s_2	$ 7 million	$4 million
s_3	$ 3 million	$4 million
s_4	$ 0	$2 million
s_5	−$ 1.5 million	$2 million

5

DECISION CRITERIA

A decision criterion is essentially a guide for determining what constitutes a good or optimal decision. Many people may feel that it is obvious what constitutes a good decision: a good decision or, more to the point, an optimal decision, is one that results in the highest payoff or least cost to the decision maker and the organization. But can this definition of an optimal decision be used in making a decision—that is, in selecting one alternative from the set of available alternatives? It could under conditions of certainty. But certainty is an unlikely condition for most decision makers. The most common situation is one of uncertain states and uncertain consequences. The previous definition could also be useful in evaluating a decision after the fact, when all the uncertainties in the situation have been resolved. But the decision maker must select an alternative and act on it while those uncertainties still exist, and at that time he doesn't know which act will result in the highest payoff or the least cost.

In decision making under uncertainty, the various consequences or payoffs for a given alternative are conditional on the occurrence of the various states. Therefore, the likelihood that a given state will occur and a specific consequence result is as important in decision making as the numerical value of the consequence. It is impossible to make a logical decision under uncertainty without dealing with the state likelihoods in some way. Each of the criteria discussed below deals with these likelihoods differently. In one, an explicit numerical assessment is made of likelihood in terms of probability. In the others, the assessment of likelihood is implicit in the criterion itself. That is, in selecting a criterion to optimize some measure of payoff, the decision maker is making an assumption about the likelihood of occurrence of the various states.

Consider the decision situation facing Electronic Devices, Inc., as described in Chapter 4. For easy reference, the payoff tables for EDI are reproduced in this chapter. Figure 5.1 describes the initial decision situation and Figure 5.2 describes the more complicated situation. In both payoff tables, it is obvious that each possible alternative has two or more conditional payoffs.

Each conditional payoff associated with an act corresponds to one of the possible states that could occur, and no single act has the best payoff for all the possible states. Selecting one act that is optimal in some sense is difficult unless we can define what constitutes optimality for the decision maker under the circumstances. Even then, having adopted some criterion of optimality, we must compare the alternatives and decide which one comes closest to meeting the criterion. Since each act encompasses a set of consequences, corresponding to the various states, such a comparison is facilitated if a *representative value* can be determined for each act. In other words, if the set of conditional consequences for each act can be reduced to a single representative value, comparing alternatives becomes a simple matter of comparing a single set of numbers, one for each act. Of course, the representative value for each act will depend on the decision criterion selected. Let's consider what some of these criteria might be.

FIGURE 5.1   Payoff table for simple EDI bid decision.

STATES	ACTS	
	a_1: bid	a_2: no bid
s_1: EDI gets contract	$350,000	$0
s_2: EDI doesn't get contract	-$ 95,000	$0

FIGURE 5.2   Final payoff table for modified EDI bid decision.

STATES	ACTS			
	a_1	a_2	a_3	a_4
s_1	$475,000	$350,000	$125,000	$0
s_2	-$ 95,000	$350,000	$125,000	$0
s_3	-$ 95,000	-$ 95,000	$125,000	$0
s_4	-$ 95,000	-$ 95,000	-$ 95,000	$0

THE CRITERION OF OPTIMISM—MAXIMAX

When considering the possible states that could occur, the decision maker should also assess his subjective feelings about their likelihood. If he is optimistic, he may want to act as though the most favorable state will occur. That is, he should select a decision criterion that will maximize his payoff under the best of all possible circumstances. This criterion is generally referred to as *maximax,* because it involves maximizing the set of maximum values. If this criterion is selected, the decision maker determines the highest payoff under each act, which he uses as the representative value for that act. He then selects that act which has the highest of the representative values.

Consider a decision situation described by the payoff table in Figure 5.3. If we let the highest payoff under each act be the representative value for the act and eliminate all the other payoffs, the table would look like this:

	a_1	a_2	a_3
s_1	$75,000		
s_2		$30,000	
s_4			$50,000

The maximum payoff possible under a_1 is $75,000 if s_1 occurs. The maximum payoff under a_2 is $30,000 if s_2 occurs, and the maximum payoff under a_3 is $50,000 if s_4 occurs. The largest of these three maximums is $75,000; therefore, under maximax, a_1 should be selected.

Consider once again the bid problem of Electronic Devices, Inc., which is described by the payoff table in Figure 5.2. Listing only the highest value under each act as the representative value of the act, the payoff table would be reduced to:

	a_1	a_2	a_3	a_4
s_1	$475,000	$350,000	$125,000	$0

It so happens in this case that the maximum payoffs all occur for the same state of nature. This is not always the case, as we have seen in the example illustrated by Figure 5.3. However, the procedure for selecting the best act is exactly the same. Since these maximums are considered to be the representative values of the acts, that act for which the representative value is the highest is selected. In the EDI example it would also be a_1. Since s_1 is the state that could result in the highest of the maximums, the decision maker acts as though s_1 were certain to occur.

The simple EDI decision situation shown in Figure 5.1 can be approached in the same way. The reader should verify that the optimal act for that situation under the maximax criterion is also a_1. Remember that when we say that an act is optimal, we are assuming some particular criterion of optimality. The optimal act under one criterion may not be the optimal act under another criterion.

This criterion of optimism, or maximax, is perfectly valid provided that it accurately reflects the decision maker's subjective assessments of the states of nature. In the EDI case, the decision maker should feel very strongly that EDI will be awarded the contract even with a high bid. And, though the intuitive aspects of decision making are important, the decision maker should certainly have substantial reasons for making this judgment.

THE CRITERION OF PESSIMISM—MAXIMIN

If there is a maximax criterion for the optimistic decision maker, it follows that there should be a different criterion for the pessimistic decision maker. This criterion of pessimism, called *maximin,* directs the decision maker to act as though the least favorable state will occur. If this accurately reflects the decision maker's feelings about the likelihoods of the various states, then he should select a criterion that will maximize his payoffs under the worst of all possible circumstances.

FIGURE 5.3 Payoff table illustrating maximax.

STATES	ACTS		
	a_1	a_2	a_3
s_1	$75,000	$15,000	-$50,000
s_2	$25,000	$30,000	-$25,000
s_3	-$25,000	$ 5,000	$ 0
s_4	-$75,000	-$ 5,000	$50,000

Under this criterion, the representative value for the act is the minimum payoff and the criterion indicates that the decision maker should choose that act that has the highest minimum. In other words, once the minimums have been established as representative values, the decision maker should select the act with the highest representative value. Consider again the payoff table in Figure 5.3. If we simply list the minimum payoff for each act and eliminate the others, the table would look like this:

	a_1	a_2	a_3
s_1			-$50,000
s_4	-$75,000	-$5,000	

Of these three minimums, the highest is $-$5,000$; therefore, act a_2 should be selected. Notice that we are dealing with negative values here and that $-$5,000$ is a larger value than $-$50,000$ or $-$75,000$.

For the EDI decision illustrated in Figure 5.2, the minimum values for all the acts correspond to state s_4. If we list these minimums and eliminate all the other payoffs, the table would appear as follows:

	a_1	a_2	a_3	a_4
s_4	-$95,000	-$95,000	-$95,000	$0

The maximum of the minimums is $0. Therefore, a_4 should be selected under this criterion, and EDI should decline to bid.

Like maximax, maximin is a valid decision criterion only if it accurately reflects the decision maker's assessment of the likelihoods of the possible states.

The reader may, at this point, criticize both of the previous criteria for being too simple and too obvious. After all, it shouldn't take much analysis for the EDI decision maker to conclude that if he believes he will be awarded the contract he should bid high, and if he thinks the contract will go to some other company he should decline to bid. This is certainly true. These two criteria simply formalize the procedure that most decision makers would use under the circumstances. However, these are not the criteria that would be used under the formal intuitive decision-making process, except in very special cases. They are introduced and described here as examples only, not as recommendations.

THE CRITERION OF NEUTRALITY—
THE UNWEIGHTED AVERAGE

Decision makers cannot always characterize themselves as being optimistic or pessimistic. In many instances, a decision maker may be entirely neutral regarding the likelihoods of the various states. This may be because he has insufficient information to make any distinction among the likelihoods or because he actually believes that all the states are equally likely to occur. Under the criterion of *neutrality*, the decision maker should act as though all the states are equally likely and determine a representative value for each act that reflects this assumption.

If all the states are weighted equally, the representative value will be the simple unweighted average of all the conditional consequences of the act or, what is essentially the same thing, the sum of all the conditional consequences. It makes no difference whether the sums or the simple averages are compared, since the average is simply the sum divided by the number of states. Be aware, however, that when positive and negative numbers are summed, the negative numbers must be subtracted. This criterion specifies that the act having the highest representative value, either total or average, should be selected.

Figures 5.4, 5.5, and 5.6 reproduce the three earlier payoff tables in this chapter with the column totals added. For the simple EDI decision in Figure 5.4, the sum of the payoffs is $255,000 for a_1 as compared with $0 for a_2. Therefore, under the criterion of neutrality, a_1 should be selected. For the more complicated EDI decision in Figure 5.5, a_2 is optimal under this criterion, since the total of $510,000 is greater than the total for

FIGURE 5.4   Payoff table for simple EDI
bid decision with totals.

STATES	ACTS	
	a_1: bid	a_2: no bid
s_1: EDI gets contract	$350,000	$0
s_2: EDI doesn't get contract	−$ 95,000	$0
	$255,000	$0

FIGURE 5.5   Payoff table for modified EDI bid decision with totals.

STATES	ACTS			
	a_1	a_2	a_3	a_4
s_1	$475,000	$350,000	$125,000	$0
s_2	−$ 95,000	$350,000	$125,000	$0
s_3	−$ 95,000	−$ 95,000	$125,000	$0
s_4	−$ 95,000	−$ 95,000	−$ 95,000	$0
	$190,000	$510,000	$280,000	$0

FIGURE 5.6   Payoff table with totals.

STATES	ACTS		
	a_1	a_2	a_3
s_1	$75,000	$15,000	−$50,000
s_2	$25,000	$30,000	−$25,000
s_3	−$25,000	$ 5,000	$ 0
s_4	−$75,000	−$ 5,000	$50,000
	$ 0	$45,000	−$25,000

any of the other acts. Finally, for the payoff table in Figure 5.6, the criterion of neutrality indicates that a_2 should be selected.

Table 5.1 compares the decisions reached under the three different criteria for each of the problems used as examples. Different criteria may result in the same decision in some cases and different decisions in others. For example, we can see from Table 5.1 that optimism and neutrality result in the same decision in the simple EDI situation, while pessimism and neutrality result in the same decision for the third example. All three criteria result in different decisions for the modified EDI situation.

TABLE 5.1 Comparison of decisions under three criteria: optimism, pessimism, and neutrality.

Decision	Optimism	Pessimism	Neutrality
Simple EDI bid decision (Figures 5.1 and 5.4)	a_1	a_2	a_1
Modified EDI bid decision (Figures 5.2 and 5.5)	a_1	a_4	a_2
Example (Figures 5.3 and 5.6)	a_1	a_2	a_2

THE EXPECTED VALUE CRITERION— THE WEIGHTED AVERAGE

The three decision criteria discussed thus far are relatively simple to apply. Under certain conditions they can be useful in helping the decision maker select an act from the set of alternatives available. These conditions have to do with the decision maker's subjective assessment of the various state likelihoods. If optimism, pessimism, or neutrality is an accurate representation of his assessment, then the decision reached by applying one of these criteria may indeed be optimal. However, these three criteria are extremely limited in expressing the decision maker's feelings about the state likelihoods. A criterion that gives the decision maker more latitude to express his feelings would be much more useful.

Up to this time, we have been using the term "likelihood" to describe the occurrence of particular states. This word is satisfactory if we limit ourselves to generalities and have no need for specific values in making our assessments. However, a more useful term is "probability," since it allows greater precision in expressing these assessments numerically. *Probability* is a numerical measure of the likelihood of occurrence of an uncertain event. In other words, probability is a numerical measure of uncertainty. If the decision maker can assess the state likelihoods in terms of numbers, he can express his subjective judgments with much greater precision than he could with words.

In developing a useful and convenient measure of probability, we will need a scale of numerical values that encompasses the two extremes of "impossibility" and "certainty." The scale we will use is a simple one. We will let a probability of 1 represent absolute certainty and a probability of 0 represent impossibility. In other words, any event with a probability of 1 is certain to occur, while an event with a probability of 0 cannot possibly occur. Furthermore, if an event is assigned a probability somewhere between 0 and 1, its exact numerical value represents the relative likelihood of its occurrence. In the formal intuitive decision-making process, probability is used as a measure of the decision maker's uncertainty about the occurrence of the various states of nature.

When a decision maker selects one of the decision criteria, he has, by his selection, made an implicit assessment of the state probabilities. For example, if he chooses the criterion of optimism, he will act as though the most preferred state of nature is certain and all other states are impossible. In terms of probability, he has assigned a probability of 1 to the preferred state and probabilities of 0 to all the others. On the other hand, if he selects the criterion of pessimism, he will act as though the least-preferred state is certain to occur and all the other states are impossible. In that case, he has assigned a probability of 1 to the least-preferred state and probabilities of 0 to all the others. Finally, if he chooses the criterion of neutrality, he is essentially assigning equal probabilities to all the possible states. So in selecting any one of these criteria, the decision maker is making a subjective assessment of probabilities even though he never explicitly states what these probabilities are.

If it is reasonable for the decision maker to assign probabilities of 0 or 1 or equal values to the states, it would seem just as reasonable for him to assign other values, not necessarily equal, to the states, as long as the assigned values represent his true feelings. By expressing his uncertainties about the states numerically, the decision maker can now deal with the uncertainty in the decision situation and utilize a much more effective criterion in making his decision. This is called the *expected value criterion*.

The expected value of an act is a weighted average of the conditional consequences, where the weights correspond to the probabilities assigned to the various states. This expected value is then used as the representative value of the act. In order to use this criterion, the decision maker must assign probability values to the individual states of nature that reflect his subjective judgments regarding their likelihood of occurring. If it should turn out that he can assign a probability value of 1 to one of the acts and 0 to all the others, then this criterion will essentially be the same as the criterion of optimism or pessimism. If he believes that all the states are indeed equally likely, then this will be the same as the criterion of neutrality. However, the expected value criterion is much more versatile than the others in that it allows the use of other and unequal probability values and thus expands the range of judgment exercised by the decision maker. It is this expected value criterion that is used in the formal intuitive decision-making process. However, methods for assessing judgmental probabilities must be discussed before we can apply this criterion to decision situations. Consequently, further explanation will have to be deferred until we discuss the measurement of uncertainty in a later chapter.

COSTS AS PAYOFFS

In all the examples used so far, the conditional consequences have been valued in terms of profit or contribution to profit. In some decision situations, however, the conditional consequences may be costs. A cost can be considered a negative contribution, and in the previous examples such values (costs or losses) were distinguished from profits by a minus sign. In a decision situation in which *all* payoffs or consequences are costs, the minus sign can be dispensed with. However, in those cases the decision criteria must be interpreted differently. While it is desirable to maximize profit, it is also desirable to minimize cost. Consequently, when a decision criterion indicates that the act with the highest representative value in terms of profit should be selected, that can now also be interpreted to mean that the act with the lowest representative value in terms of cost should be selected.

Under optimism, instead of maximizing the maximum profit we minimize the minimum cost, and maximax becomes minimin. Under pessimism, instead of maximizing the minimum profit, we minimize the maximum cost, and the criterion is called minimax instead of maximin. Under neutrality, the act with the *lowest* average or total cost is the one that should be selected.

The Granger Case

Let's return to the Granger case described in the previous chapter. Paul Granger must decide whether to accept or reject Southeastern Mutual's offer of $600,000 for his land. The states in this situation are the future actions of the state highway department regarding a proposed expressway route. The situation was described by the payoff table in Figure 4.5. What is Granger's optimal decision under the criteria of optimism, pessimism, and neutrality?

If Granger is optimistic and believes that the expressway route will be approved, he will want to maximize the maximum payoffs. The maximums for each act are:

	a_1	a_2
s_1	$600,000	$750,000

Since the maximum of these two values is $750,000, Granger should choose a_2 and reject the offer of the insurance company. Note that this is the decision Granger would make if he were certain that the expressway route would be approved.

If Granger is pessimistic, he will want to maximize the minimum payoffs. In that case, he would consider only the minimum payoffs for each act:

	a_1	a_2
s_2	$600,000	$475,000

Since the maximum of the minimums is $600,000, Granger should choose a_1 and accept the offer of the insurance company. Note that this is the decision he would make if he were certain that the expressway route would not be approved.

If Granger is neither optimistic nor pessimistic and has no reason to believe that one of the states is more likely to occur than the other, he will adopt the criterion of neutrality. In that case, he would be concerned with the value of the sums or the simple averages of the payoffs under each act:

	a_1	a_2
Sums	$1,200,000	$1,225,000
Averages	$ 600,000	$ 612,500

Since the values under a_2 are greater than those under a_1, Granger should choose a_2 and reject the offer.

The Thompson Case

Frank Thompson must choose between six alternatives: purchase one through five lots or purchase none at all. The payoff table for this decision situation was illustrated in Figure 4.6. Under the criterion of optimism, Thompson should consider only the set of maximum payoffs:

	a_0	a_1	a_2	a_3	a_4	a_5
s_5	$0	$17,000	$34,000	$51,000	$68,000	$85,000

The maximum of these maximums is $85,000; therefore, Thompson should select a_5 and purchase five lots.

Under the criterion of pessimism, he should consider only the set of minimums, which are:

	a_0	a_1	a_2	a_3	a_4	a_5
s_0	$0	-$78,000	-$156,000	-$234,000	-$312,000	-$390,000

The maximum of these minimums is $0; therefore, Thompson should select a_0 and purchase no lots.

Under neutrality, the representative set would consist of the column sums or averages. The column sums are:

	a_0	a_1	a_2	a_3	a_4	a_5
Sums	$0	$7,000	-$115,000	-$264,000	-$542,000	-$915,000

Since the maximum of these representative values is $7,000, Thompson should purchase one lot.

The Eastways Case

The Eastways decision involved an initial choice among three acts:

> a_1: accept the new line and establish a separate division
> a_2: accept the new line and use the existing organization
> a_3: reject the new line

Since a_3 turned out to be an inferior act, the final decision was simply a choice between a_1 and a_2. The payoff table for this decision was shown in Figure 4.8.

Under maximax, the set of representative values is:

	a_1	a_2
s_7	$300,000	$230,000

The maximum of the maximums is $300,000; therefore a_1 should be selected.

Under maximin, the set of representative values is:

	a_1	a_2
s_1	−$110,000	$20,000

Since the maximum of the minimums is $20,000, a_2 should be selected.

Under neutrality, with sums as the representative values, a_2 should again be selected:

	a_1	a_2
Sums	$690,000	$875,000

The Thermocal Case

Regardless of how complicated a decision situation is, once it has been described with a payoff table, any of the decision criteria we have discussed can be easily applied in arriving at a decision. The final payoff table for the Thermocal case was shown in Figure 4.10. Considerable analysis was required to reduce the complicated statement of the problem to the representation in the payoff table. However, under maximax, maximin, and neutrality, the representative values are:

Maximax

	a_1	a_2
s_1	$11 million	$8 million

Maximin

	a_1	a_2
s_5	−$1.5 million	$2 million

Neutrality

	a_1	a_2
Sums	$19.5 million	$20 million

The optimal decisions under each of these criteria are maximax, a_1; maximin, a_2; and neutrality, a_2.

6

DESCRIBING THE DECISION
SITUATION—DECISION TREES

The payoff table is an extremely useful device for describing situations that require a single decision at a specific point in time. Such situations are called single-stage decision problems. There are, however, situations that involve a sequence of decisions made at different points in time where the consequence of each subsequent decision depends not only on the states of nature but also on the previous decision. This type of situation is called a multistage decision problem. The payoff table is not a useful device for describing that type of decision situation.

As we saw in Chapter 2, a decision problem has three components: alternatives, states of nature, and consequences. The alternatives are under the full control of the decision maker. That is, the decision maker is free to select any one alternative from the set of available alternatives. The states, on the other hand, are beyond the control of the decision maker and under the control of "nature." The third component, the consequences, results from the choice of an act by the decision maker and the selection of a state by nature. This sequence of events can be displayed with a tree diagram or *decision tree*.

In such a diagram, all choices are represented by lines or branches that emanate from an intersection called a node. When the branches represent the alternatives available to the decision maker, the node is called a *decision node* and is represented by a small square or rectangle, □. A decision node is illustrated in Figure 6.1. When the branches issuing from a node represent states of nature, the node is called a *chance node* and is represented by a small circle or oval, ○. A chance node is illustrated in Figure 6.2.

A decision tree links these branches, decision nodes, and chance nodes together to describe the decision situation. Any decision situation that can be described with a payoff table can also be described with a decision tree. However, the decision tree can also be used for multistage decision situations, which cannot be described with payoff tables. Let's look first at the decision tree for single-stage decision situations, which we have already described with payoff tables.

DECISION TREES FOR SINGLE-STAGE DECISIONS

Consider the simple EDI decision situation illustrated earlier in Figure 4.1 and reproduced here as Figure 6.3. This is a single-stage, two-action problem requiring a choice between two alternatives—a_1: bid, and a_2: decline to bid. The states of nature are s_1: EDI gets contract, and s_2: EDI doesn't get contract. The decision tree description of this situation is shown in Figure 6.4.

The first node in a decision tree is always a decision node. Issuing from the decision node is a branch for each alternative available to the decision maker. At the end of each branch is a chance node, and issuing from each chance node is a branch for each of the states of nature in the problem. At the end of each branch issuing from the chance node is the value corresponding

FIGURE 6.1 Decision node.   FIGURE 6.2 Chance node.

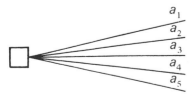

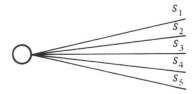

FIGURE 6.3 Payoff table for simple EDI bid decision.

STATES	ACTS	
	a_1: bid	a_2: no bid
s_1: EDI gets contract	$350,000	$0
s_2: EDI doesn't get contract	−$ 95,000	$0

to the conditional consequence of the act and the state. In a sense, the decision tree is like a roadmap. If the decision maker selects a_1 and nature chooses s_1, the path leads to the consequence $350,000.

Now let's look at the more complicated EDI decision, origi-

FIGURE 6.4 Decision tree for simple EDI bid decision.

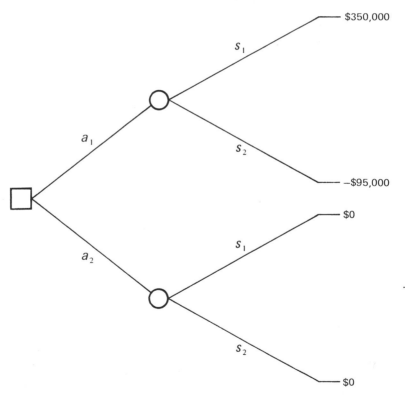

nally described in Figure 4.4 and reproduced here as Figure 6.5. The alternatives are:

a_1: bid high
a_2: bid moderate
a_3: bid low
a_4: no bid

The states are:

s_1: EDI gets contract with high, moderate, or low bid
s_2: EDI gets contract with moderate or low bid
s_3: EDI gets contract with low bid
s_4: EDI doesn't get contract

The decision tree description of this situation is provided in Figure 6.6. The first node is a decision node from which four branches issue, each branch corresponding to one of the possible alternatives. Each of these branches terminates at a chance node. Issuing from each chance node is a branch corresponding to each of the possible states. Each of the state branches terminates in the conditional consequence resulting from that state and the appropriate alternative.

The decision tree representation of the situation in Figure 6.6 can now be compared with the payoff table in Figure 6.5. The conditional payoffs at the end of each branch of the decision tree correspond to the values at the intersection of the appropriate act and state in the payoff table. In comparing these two descriptive devices, we can see that the payoff table is more compact and easier to comprehend. It is also easier to construct. For these reasons, the payoff table is generally preferred for describing a one-stage decision problem. The decision tree be-

FIGURE 6.5   Final payoff table for modified EDI bid decision.

STATES	ACTS			
	a_1	a_2	a_3	a_4
s_1	$475,000	$350,000	$125,000	$0
s_2	−$ 95,000	$350,000	$125,000	$0
s_3	−$ 95,000	−$ 95,000	$125,000	$0
s_4	−$ 95,000	−$ 95,000	−$ 95,000	$0

FIGURE 6.6 Decision tree for modified EDI bid decision.

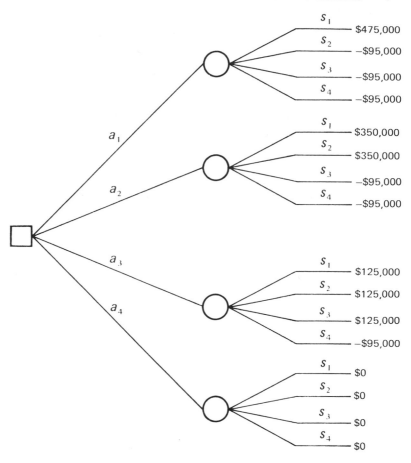

comes useful in multistage decision situations, where payoff tables are not applicable.

DECISION TREES FOR MULTISTAGE DECISIONS

In a multistage decision situation, two or more decisions must be made at different points in time. When this type of situation is described with a decision tree, the diagram should show each set of alternatives in the order in which they must occur as well as all sets of uncertain states in the order in which the uncertainties can be resolved. With multistage decision situations, it is helpful to place dates on the decision tree to keep the sequence of events in their proper order.

Several dates are important in describing the decision situation. We have already defined the cutoff date as the future date by which all the consequences of the decision situation can be evaluated. The decision date is the date at which an irrevocable choice must be made among some set of alternatives. In this definition, the term "irrevocable" is important. If any choice can be revoked at a later date *without penalty* to the decision maker, a true decision has not been made. In a multistage decision situation, two or more decision dates can be noted at each decision node. Finally, the date at which the uncertainties about a given set of states of nature can be resolved is called the *resolution date.* The resolution date for each set of states can also be noted on the decision tree at each chance node.

Whenever a decision date precedes the resolution date for some set of states, the uncertainties about that set of states must be considered in making that decision. When a resolution date precedes a decision date, that particular decision will be unaffected by the uncertainties about that set of states since they will already be resolved by the time the decision must be made.

A decision tree description of a multistage decision situation consists of a sequence of decision nodes and chance nodes joined by the branches representing the alternatives and the states. The decision dates are entered at each decision node and then checked to be sure that all the alternatives branching from that node are available at that date and that an irrevocable choice of one of those alternatives must be made at that date. The resolution dates are also entered at each chance node and then checked to be sure that all the uncertainties about those states can be resolved at that date. Finally, the entire decision diagram should be checked to be sure that the proper chronological order is maintained when reading from left to right. We will illustrate the multistage decision situation with the Granger case, first discussed in Chapter 4.

To review that case briefly, Paul Granger has received an offer of $600,000 from the Southeastern Mutual Life Insurance Company for the purchase of 25 acres of land. Granger must make an immediate decision either to accept the offer or to

FIGURE 6.7   Payoff table for Granger land decision.

STATES	ACTS	
	a_1: accept	a_2: reject
s_1: route approved	$600,000	$750,000
s_2: route not approved	$600,000	$475,000

reject it in anticipation of selling the land at a later date to the state highway department for $750,000. The sale to the state is contingent on the approval of an expressway route over the land. If the route is not approved, Granger can subdivide the land and sell it as individual building lots. He estimates a net profit of $475,000 from this last alternative. The uncertainty in this situation relates to the approval of the expressway route. Granger must reply to Southeastern's offer within 72 hours, a period that expires on April 1, 1980. Consequently, April 1, 1980 is the decision date for that immediate decision.

The state's decision on the expressway route will not be known for 60 days. Therefore, the resolution date for the states in the problem is May 31, 1980. The cutoff date for the evaluation of all consequences was specified as one year from the decision date, or April 1, 1981. As it stands, this is still a one-stage decision. The payoff table describing this situation was presented in Figure 4.5 and is reproduced here as Figure 6.7. The same situation is also described by the decision tree in Figure 6.8.

PRUNING THE DECISION TREE

Because decision trees can get quite complicated, it is always helpful to prune or simplify a tree by eliminating branches whenever possible. Notice that on the "accept" branch of the tree in Figure 6.8 the payoff is exactly the same whether or not the expressway route is approved. Consequently, it isn't necessary to draw the chance node and its two branches after the "accept" decision. That portion of the tree can be eliminated and the "accept" branch can be shown as leading directly to a payoff of $600,000. The pruned decision tree for this situation is shown in

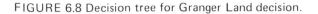

FIGURE 6.8 Decision tree for Granger Land decision.

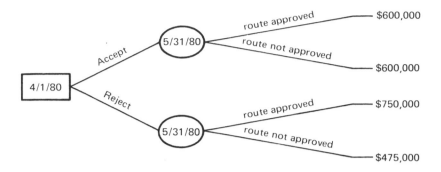

Figure 6.9. Notice that the chance node and the branches issuing from it are still necessary for the "reject" decision because these states will affect the payoff resulting from that alternative.

Now let's turn this into a multistage decision situation by providing Paul Granger with an additional alternative. Suppose that, instead of demanding a response to its offer within 72 hours, Southeastern Mutual gives Granger the option of postponing his decision until June 1. By that time, the decision on the expressway route will be known. However, the cost of exercising this option is $100,000. That is, if Granger postpones his decision and then decides to sell to Southeastern on June 1, the offer is reduced from $600,000 to $500,000. This additional alternative changes the situation from a single-stage problem to a two-stage problem with two decision dates: April 1 and June 1.

FIGURE 6.9 Pruned decision tree for Granger Land decision.

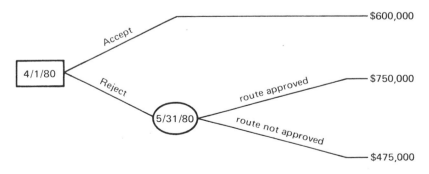

The resolution date for the uncertain states (the expressway approval) is May 31, which follows the first decision date but precedes the second one. This new decision situation is diagrammed in Figure 6.10. The top part of the figure is identical to Figure 6.9. The bottom part corresponds to the new alternative in the situation.

Is it possible to simplify the tree diagram still further? Since the top part has already been pruned, we should focus our attention on the new alternative, "postpone." This portion of the decision diagram is isolated in Figure 6.11. Notice that the first decision date of April 1 precedes the resolution date, while the second decision date of June 1 follows it. This chronological

FIGURE 6.10 Decision tree for Granger case with option to postpone.

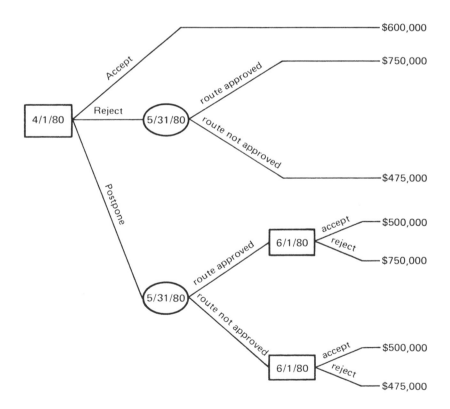

FIGURE 6.11 Postpone branch of Granger decision situation.

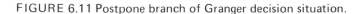
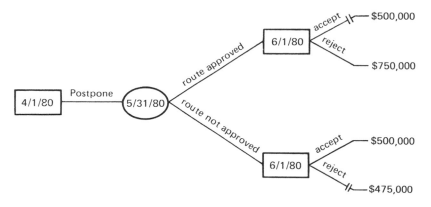

order is shown clearly on the decision tree. If the initial decision is to postpone, the next decision (to accept or reject Southeastern Mutual's offer) does not have to be made until June 1—after the uncertainty about the expressway route has been resolved. Therefore, at the decision node labeled 6/1/80 following the "route approved" branch, the choice between the two alternatives can be made under conditions of certainty. If the route is approved, the "reject" alternative is clearly superior to the "accept" alternative, since a $750,000 payoff is better than a $500,000 payoff. Consequently, the "accept" alternative should be eliminated from the diagram at that point. This can be shown by drawing two short lines across the branch, as illustrated in Figure 6.11.

On the other hand, if the expressway route is not approved, a decision must be made at the node labeled 6/1/80 following the "route not approved" branch. Given that the route is not approved, the "accept" alternative is superior to "reject," since a $500,000 payoff is better than a $475,000 payoff. Therefore, at this point on the diagram the "reject" alternative should be eliminated and two short lines drawn across that branch. The revised "postpone" branch is shown in Figure 6.12 with the inferior alternatives eliminated. The decision tree for the entire Granger decision situation is shown in Figure 6.13 with the pruned "postpone" branch included.

It might seem as though the decision tree in Figure 6.12 should be the final description of the Granger decision situation. However, this tree can be pruned even further by eliminating what now shows up as a clearly inferior act. Remember that a

FIGURE 6.12 Postpone branch of Granger decision situation after pruning.

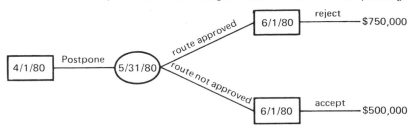

FIGURE 6.13 Decision tree for Granger decision situation with pruned postpone branch.

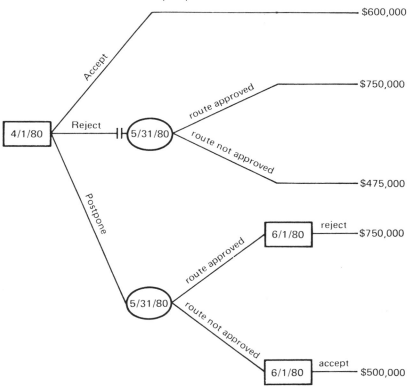

dominant act is one for which the conditional consequences are at least as good as those of another act for all states of nature and better than those of the other act for at least one state of nature. Now compare the "reject" and "postpone" alternatives that issue from the decision node labeled 4/1/80. If the expressway route is approved, the payoffs are identical for both alternatives—that is, $750,000. However, if the route is not approved, the payoff for the "postpone" alternative is $500,000 as compared with a payoff of $475,000 for the "reject" alternative. By definition, the "postpone" alternative dominates the "reject" alternative and "reject" is an inferior act that should be eliminated. This is shown in Figure 6.13 by the two lines drawn across the "reject" branch. The completely pruned decision tree for the Granger case is shown in Figure 6.14.

We can now compare the decision tree in Figure 6.14 with the one in Figure 6.10. It is obvious that the description of the decision situation has been simplified considerably by judicious pruning of the tree. This was accomplished by a series of succes-

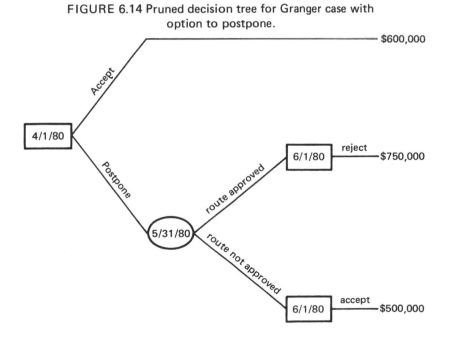

FIGURE 6.14 Pruned decision tree for Granger case with option to postpone.

sive approximations, since it is extremely difficult to jump from the initial statement of a multistage decision situation to its final representation in a single step.

It is still not possible, at this stage, to determine what course of action Granger should take, but his choices have been clarified considerably. They are now either "accept Southeastern Mutual's offer immediately" or "postpone the decision until June 1 and then, if the route is approved, reject the offer; otherwise accept the offer." The latter alternative, which consists of a sequence of acts conditioned by the way the state uncertainties are resolved, is called a *decision strategy*.

The Granger Case—Further Complications

Let's add another complication to the Granger case to show how additional factors can be handled with the decision tree. Suppose that, before the initial decision date of April 1, Paul Granger learns that a tract of 100 acres adjacent to his own land is being considered by the Tristate Development Company as a site for a new shopping mall. The mall, if constructed, would contain several specialty shops, two department stores, a theater, restaurants, a bank, and a variety of other shops. If Tristate goes ahead with its plans, the value of Granger's property as residential lots will increase by at least 10%. More specifically, if the mall is constructed, Granger estimates that his profit from the sale of building lots will be $525,000 rather than the $475,000 he originally estimated without the mall. Granger immediately calls the president of Tristate, who verifies that the mall project is under consideration but that a decision will not be made until July 1.

This additional factor—the possibility of the mall—should be considered in Granger's decision. To see how this relates to the other factors in the situation, we need to construct a new decision tree, as shown in Figure 6.15. Notice that the initial "reject" alternative, which was eliminated from the decision tree in Figure 6.14 as an inferior act, has been reinstated in the new diagram. At this point we cannot be sure how the new factor affects this alternative and whether it will still be an inferior act under the new situation.

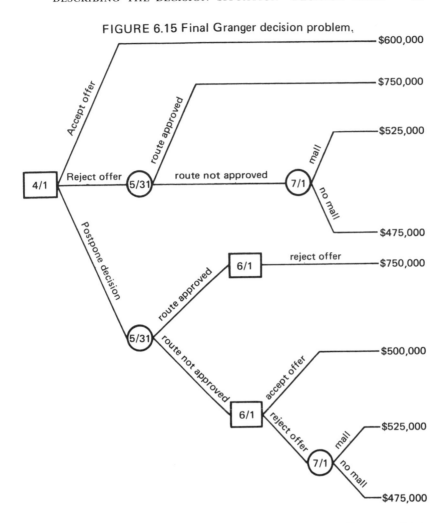

FIGURE 6.15 Final Granger decision problem,

The first decision date for Granger is still April 1, at which time he must choose among the following alternatives:

Accept Southeastern Mutual's offer
Reject Southeastern Mutual's offer
Postpone the decision

If he accepts the offer on April 1, none of the future events will have any effect on his payoff, which is simply $600,000. However, if he rejects the offer on April 1, two sets of uncertain states will affect his payoff. These are the states relating to the expressway route and the states relating to the mall. The resolution dates for these uncertain states are May 31 and July 1 respectively. If the expressway route is approved, Granger's payoff will be $750,000. If the route is not approved, it will be $525,000 if the mall is built or $475,000 if the mall is not built.

If Granger chooses the "postpone" alternative on April 1, he is faced with a second decision date on June 1. The resolution date for the expressway route precedes the second decision date but the resolution date for the mall follows it. We have previously determined that if the route is approved Granger should reject the offer from Southeastern Mutual, since the $750,000 payoff from the state highway department is greater than Southeastern's offer for the property. However, if the route is not approved, Granger must decide whether to accept or reject that offer on June 1. If he accepts the offer, his payoff is $500,000. If he rejects the offer, his payoff is contingent on the set of uncertain states relating to the mall. If the mall is built, his payoff is $525,000; if it is not built, his payoff is only $475,000.

The decision situation outlined in the previous two paragraphs is much more simply and concisely described by the decision tree in Figure 6.15. Once again, it is important to emphasize that while the decision tree is an extremely useful device for describing a decision situation, it does not, by itself, constitute a solution to the decision maker's dilemma. Like a roadmap, the decision tree provides the decision maker with a clear picture of the terrain ahead. It also enables him to eliminate from consideration some of the clearly inferior routes. But it does not automatically tell him which of the remaining routes is the best. For this, the decision maker needs some criterion of choice, and although we have already discussed several decision criteria, the one used in the formal intuitive method has not yet been explained.

The Thermocal Case—Further Complications

The Thermocal decision situation was described by the payoff table in Figure 4.10, which is reproduced here as Figure 6.16. A decision tree description of the case is presented in Figure 6.17.

FIGURE 6.16 Payoff table for single-stage Thermocal decision.

STATES	ACTS	
	a_1: solar power	a_2: advertising
s_1: economy good	$11 million	$8 million
s_2: economy fair and no competition	$ 7 million	$4 million
s_3: economy fair and competition	$ 3 million	$4 million
s_4: economy poor and no competition	$ 0	$2 million
s_5: economy poor and competition	−$1.5 million	$2 million

To summarize the case briefly, on August 15 the president of Thermocal must make a decision, in the form of a recommendation to the board of directors, on whether to proceed with the development of a new solar power system, initiate a new advertising campaign, or maintain the status quo. After some discussion, the status quo alternative was determined to be inferior to the others and was eliminated from consideration. This last alternative is shown on the decision tree with a double line through the a_3 branch to indicate that it is no longer being considered in the decision.

If the president decides to develop the solar power system, a prototype will be completed by January 15, 1983, at a cost of $2.5 million. Delivery of commercial systems can begin by January 15, 1984. An additional $500,000 will be spent on advertising and promotion during the year following development of the prototype. If the advertising alternative is chosen, the program will begin on January 1, 1982, and continue for two years. The cutoff date for both alternatives is December 31, 1984, and the payoffs represent contributions to profit.

Now, let's suppose that some of the uncertainties about the states of nature can be resolved on June 15, 1982. On this date, a firm of economic consultants retained by Thermocal will deliver a forecast covering the period January 1, 1983, through December 31, 1984. Although these forecasts are not 100% accurate, Thermocal has found them to be extremely reliable in the past. Consequently, on June 15, 1982, Thermocal believes that the major uncertainties about the economy will be resolved. However, the uncertainties about the competition will still exist. The presence or absence of competition will not be known until

FIGURE 6.17 Decision tree for single-stage Thermocal decision.

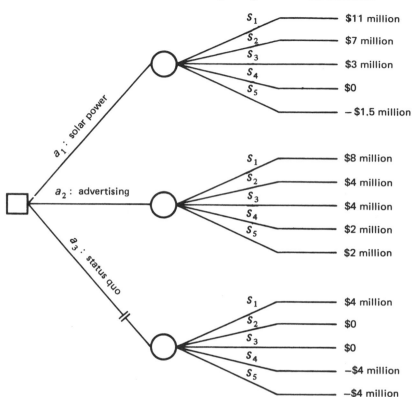

the time that the system is ready to be sold commercially—that is, January 15, 1984.

By June 15, 1982, the resolution date for uncertainties about the economy, Thermocal will have spent approximately $1 million on prototype development. This is still considerably less than the $3 million that would be spent if the project were completed and the system marketed. Therefore, on June 15, 1982 it is possible for Thermocal to reconsider the decision to develop the system and then either continue or cancel the project. If Thermocal decides to cancel, the $1 million spent up to that time will be a total loss. Thus June 15, 1982, is not only a resolution date for the economy but also a second decision date: at that time, Thermocal can choose between continuing or canceling the solar power project. This has now become a two-stage decision situation. Let's construct a new decision tree to describe it.

Since the "status quo" branch was eliminated earlier as an inferior alternative, we have only two of the initial branches to consider. Let's look first at the solar power branch. The first decision date, 8/15/81, is followed by a chance node at 6/15/82, the resolution date for the economy. From this node a branch issues corresponding to the three economic states of "good," "fair," and "poor." As soon as these state uncertainties are resolved, Thermocal can make a decision to continue with the project or to cancel it. Consequently, each of these state branches will lead to another decision node. Since this second decision will be made after the economic uncertainties are resolved, the decision node will be to the right of the chance node on the diagram.

In order to avoid confusion about the proper sequence, we will make this second decision date June 16, 1982, one day after the resolution date. At this second decision node, Thermocal must choose between the alternatives "continue" and "cancel." Each of these two branches will lead to another chance node, at which time the uncertainties about the competition will be resolved. Since these states relate to the presence or absence of competition at the time Thermocal begins to market its system, the uncertainties will not be resolved until the system goes on the market—that is, January 15, 1984. From each of these last chance nodes, branches corresponding to "competition" and "no competition" will lead to the final payoffs. This portion of the decision tree is illustrated in Figure 6.18.

The next step is, of course, to prune the tree in order to simplify the diagram. Starting at the top, you will notice that if the economy is good the alternative "cancel" is clearly inferior to "continue." The payoffs for both alternatives are not affected by the presence or absence of competition, and a profit of $11 million is certainly superior to a loss of $1 million. Therefore, if the economy is good, the alternative "cancel" can be eliminated. The chance node at 1/15/84 can also be eliminated, since the presence or absence of competition will have no effect on the payoffs on this branch.

If the economy is fair, the "cancel" alternative can again be

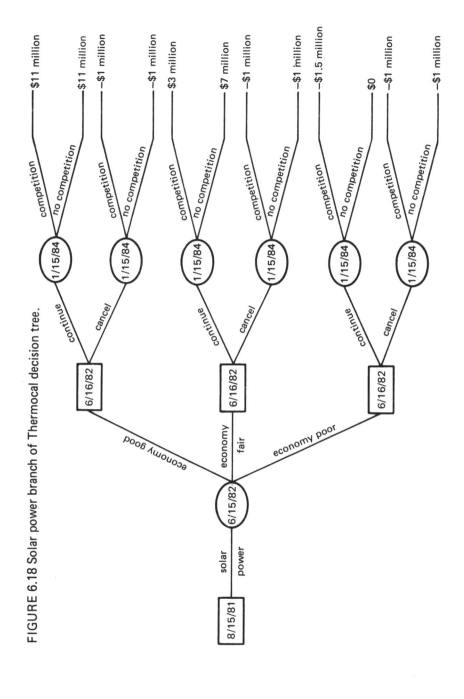

FIGURE 6.18 Solar power branch of Thermocal decision tree.

eliminated. Continuing the project can only result in profits (either $3 million or $7 million, depending on the competition), while canceling can only result in a loss of $1 million.

If the economy is poor, the "continue" alternative leads to a payoff of either −$1.5 million or $0, depending on the competition. The "cancel" alternative leads to a loss of $1 million regardless of the competition. However, until the uncertainty about the competition is resolved, neither branch can be eliminated. The solar power branch after pruning is shown in Figure 6.19.

If the advertising alternative is chosen on the initial decision date of 8/15/81, the consequences will be affected by the economy but not by the presence or absence of competition in the solar power field. Also, there are no future decisions to be made. The complete, pruned decision tree for the Thermocal case is shown in Figure 6.20.

SUMMARY OF DIAGRAMMING PROCEDURE

1. Identify the immediate or first decision and specify the date at which that decision must be made.
2. List the set of alternatives available to the decision maker at the first decision date, from which an irrevocable choice must be made.
3. Specify the cutoff date for the immediate decision. This is the latest date at which all the consequences of the decision will be evaluated.
4. Identify and list all the uncertain states of nature that can directly affect the consequences of the initial decision and specify their resolution date.
5. Identify and list all the future decisions that can affect the consequences of the initial decision and specify the decision date for each.
6. Identify and list all the states of nature that provide information about and/or affect the consequences of each future decision and specify their resolution dates.
7. Begin the tree diagram with the initial decision node and enter all other chance and decision nodes with branches in chronological order from left to right.

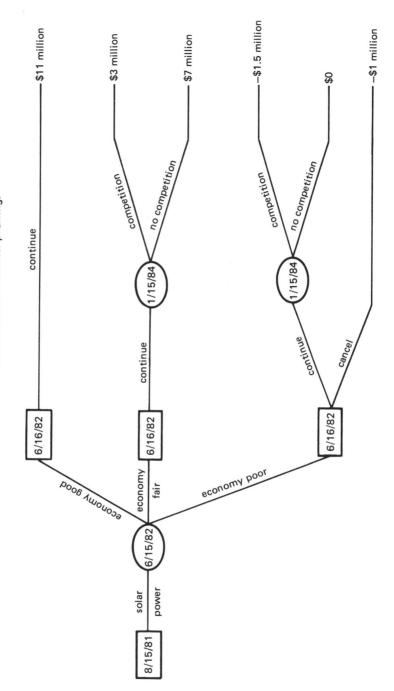

FIGURE 6.19 Solar power branch of Thermocal decision tree after pruning.

FIGURE 6.20 Complete decision tree for Thermocal multistage decision situation.

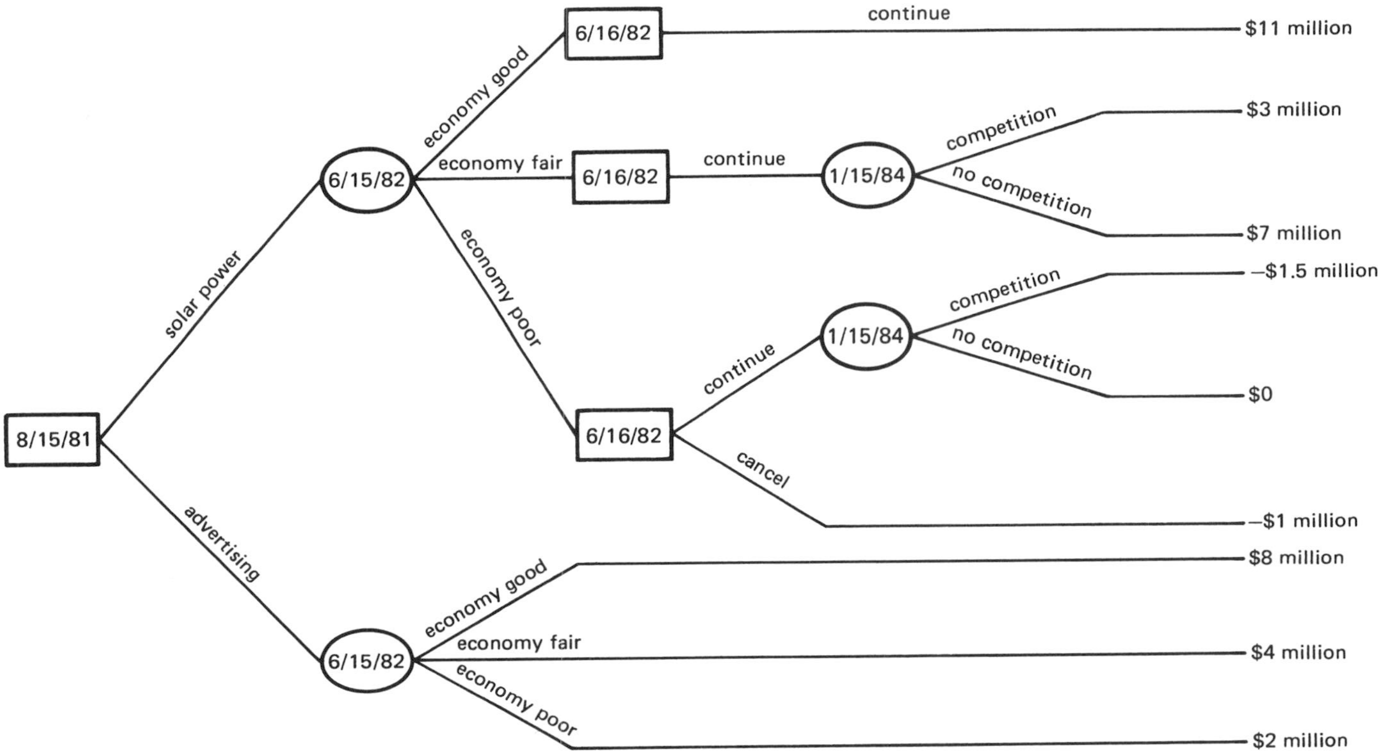

8. Enter the decision dates and the resolution dates at the appropriate decision and chance nodes.
9. Check the diagram to be sure that the chronological order of occurrences is correct.
10. Enter the payoffs, in terms of net contribution, at the termination of each branch of the tree.
11. Check the diagram for and eliminate inferior alternatives.
12. Check the diagram for and eliminate inconsequential states.

Generally, as decision situations increase in complexity, the final decision tree must be obtained through a series of approximations. It may also be necessary to consider the individual alternatives or branches separately rather than attempting to construct the entire tree at one time.

7

MEASURING UNCERTAINTY

The purpose of the formal intuitive method of decision making is to provide a logical, systematic, and consistent procedure for making optimal decisions under conditions of uncertainty. To use the method successfully, it is necessary first to describe the decision situation and all its pertinent components in a clear, concise, correct, and complete manner and then to select a criterion for making a choice among the courses of action available. The techniques for describing the situation and some of the decision criteria have already been discussed thoroughly. However, discussion of the most important decision-making criterion, the expected value criterion, was postponed, because it requires that the decision maker express these uncertainties about the states of nature as a value on some numerical scale. So far, we have had no method for doing this.

The three decision criteria we have already considered—criteria for optimists, pessimists, and neutralists—were devised in an attempt to make the best possible choices under conditions of uncertainty. However, none of these criteria dealt with the problem of uncertainty except in a very superficial way. Although any one of these criteria might occasionally lead to an optimal decision, it should be fairly obvious that none of them would provide a consistent guide to decision making that could be considered satisfactory. Successful decision makers do not generally use these criteria. Any consistently useful criterion for making successful choices must consider and accommodate the state probabilities, which have a a significant effect on the consequences or payoffs in decision situations of this type.

However, as we have seen, even the criteria of optimism, pessimism, and neutrality make some implicit assumptions about the uncertain states of nature. By selecting any one of these three criteria, the decision maker is expressing his subjective feelings about the likelihood of occurrence of the possible states in a rough and very general way. For instance, the criterion of optimism assumes that out of all possible states that could occur, the best or most favorable will happen. If this assumption were valid, then the choice determined by this strategy would, of course, be advantageous. Unfortunately, chance doesn't behave so predictably. To assume that the best will always happen and to act accordingly can have disastrous results.

The same can be said for the criterion of pessimism. This strategy assumes that the worst of the possible occurrences will always happen. Again, although preparing for the worst may be an admirable trait, consistently behaving in this manner is not the best way to attain success. The strategy of neutrality assumes that every possible event is just as likely to occur as every other one. There are times when this may be true. However, we also know that in most chance situations this is unlikely.

The expected value criterion, which is used in the formal intuitive method, provides the decision maker with much more latitude in expressing his subjective feelings about the likelihoods of the possible states. This criterion utilizes a quantitative measure of likelihood which we call probability.

As mentioned in Chapter 5, probability is expressed on a scale of numerical values that encompass the extremes of "impossibility" and "certainty." On this scale, the number 1 represents certainty and the number 0 represents impossibility. Any number between 0 and 1 then represents the relative likelihood of the event or state occurring. The decision maker's problem is to determine what exact value best expresses his subjective assessment of the relative likelihood. In order to solve this problem, we must first consider the nature and characteristics of the probability measure.

THE NATURE OF PROBABILITY

Philosophers and mathematicians have long disagreed about the nature of probability. Basically, the two sides of the argument are that (1) probability is a state of the universe, and (2) probability is a state of mind or belief. Those who subscribe to the first view are generally called objectivists, and those who subscribe to the second are called subjectivists. The implications of these two viewpoints are important to the decision maker.

If probability is a state of the universe, then every event has a fixed and definite probability of occurring, and that probability is determined by physical factors in the external world. If it were possible to identify, observe, and precisely measure all these external factors, we should be able to determine the exact probability of any event. In the absence of that ability, we must use our imperfect knowledge and observational ability to estimate what that true probability is. Our estimate may be a good one or a poor one, but in either case the difference between our estimate and the true probability is an error.

There are, of course, certain events for which the true probability can be determined. For example, the probability of getting a head on the single toss of a fair coin and the probability that a 6 will come up on the roll of a true die are values that can be easily determined. Even with no prior knowledge of probability, most decision makers can see that the first probability is 1/2 and the second is 1/6. However, there are many events for which the exact probability can never be determined.

A common example is the weather. Most weather forecasts include a prediction of the probability of rain tomorrow. How is this probability determined? From an objective viewpoint, it is determined by many forces in the universe, such as the wind speed and direction, the temperature, the humidity, and so on. If meteorologists could identify all the factors that influence tomorrow's weather and could measure them with absolute precision, they would be able to determine the true probability of rain. In the absence of such perfect knowledge and precise measurement capabilities, meteorologists can only estimate what this true probability might be.

If, on the other hand, we adopt the subjective viewpoint, then the probability of an event is simply an individual's subjective belief in the occurrence or nonoccurrence of the event. This means that if you believe that the probability of rain tomorrow is .6 and you are willing to act in a manner that is consistent with your assessment, then .6 is the true probability of that event as far as you are concerned. If I, on the other hand, believe that the probability of rain is .7 and am willing to act accordingly, then .7 is the true probability of that event as far as I am concerned.

Does this mean that under the subjective viewpoint the individual is free to pick any numerical value between 0 and 1 as the probability of an event—and that number then becomes the true probability of the event, at least as far as he is concerned? In a sense, this is true. However, the probability assessment should be a reasonable one that is consistent with all available evidence concerning that event. As stated earlier, not only should the decision maker believe in his subjective probability value; he should also be willing to act in a manner that is consistent with that belief. The true measure of belief is commitment. And in managerial decision making that commitment is resources under risk. It is easy to say, "I believe that the probability of such-and-such an event occurring is .8." But what, or how much, are you willing to risk on the strength of that belief? In decision making, risks are unavoidable. The decision maker should minimize these risks by assessing the probabilities of the states bearing on his decision situation in a reasonable manner, using all the information available to him.

For example, if we are tossing a fair coin and betting substantial amounts on the outcome of each toss, it would certainly be unwise to assess the probability of a head as .9. The decision maker, who must decide when and how much to bet, is certainly free to make any probability assessment that appears reasonable. But if the coin clearly has a head on one side and a tail on the other, a probability of .9 for the event "head" would not appear to be very reasonable. If the decision maker persists in acting as though .9 were the probability of a head, he might lose quite a lot of money. On the other hand, if the decision maker observes 100 tosses of the same coin which result in 95 heads and 5 tails, it would also be unrealistic to insist that the probability of a head is .5.

Subjective assessments of probability must be consistent with a reasonable interpretation of the evidence. Since managerial decision makers are assumed to be reasonable, we use the subjective viewpoint in assessing probability in the formal intuitive method.

SUBJECTIVE INFORMATION

Subjective information is information or knowledge that we cannot immediately verify or substantiate with objective or empirical evidence.

We all receive information constantly. How many times in a discussion of politics or business do we make statements based on something we read or heard? If we were asked to verify exactly where our information came from, we would be unable to cite specific references, dates, and page numbers, and yet we are sure that the information is correct. We simply know it. We read, we observe, we hear. The information thus obtained is valid. We may know something without being exactly certain how we know it. Sometimes this is called intuition.

Basically the weakness of such subjective information is not that it can't be substantiated (except when we are trying to win a debate or an argument). The weakness lies in its interpretation!

We receive information from many different sources in the environment. Some of the sources *are* empirical, such as written reports from subordinates. But many are not empirical: observation of activities, overheard conversation, impressions, and so forth. All these are evaluated by us to some extent and stored away as knowledge. This information is information in the same sense as any empirical data we receive, and it is useful or useless, good or bad, valid or invalid depending on our interpretation of it.

For example, a person could walk into the operating room of a hospital and observe a surgical procedure. Without talking to anyone or asking questions, he could receive many impressions. However, not being a surgeon or even a doctor and knowing nothing about operating room procedures, he would be unable to interpret these impressions and provide a valid assessment of what he observed. His evaluation would probably be totally erroneous. In such an instance, his subjective information could be less than worthless.

But if a production manager with years of experience walks into a manufacturing plant and observes operations, his subjective evaluation of his impressions based on that experience is probably extremely accurate. And if it happens to be his own plant and his own operation, then his subjective store of data represents some very real and valuable information that should be used in making decisions about that operation.

Every manager uses subjective information in making minor decisions. The manager recognizes the value of subjective information in those instances and probably refers to it as experience, know-how, or intuition. The fact is that such subjective information is also valuable in making major decisions. However, in order to use it effectively, the manager must have some consistent method for converting the information into a form usable in decision making. This is essentially what formal intuitive decision making is all about.

CHARACTERISTICS OF PROBABILITY

The numerical measure of the probability of an event or state has certain characteristics and its use must be guided by a set of rules. The same rules apply whether the probability was obtained subjectively or was computed from empirical data. In assigning probability values to states in a particular decision situation, the decision maker must be sure that the values reflect his subjective assessment of the likelihood of each state occurring and that his assessment is consistent with the evidence available to him. In addition, the decision maker must be guided by the following rules:

Rule 1. Every probability value must be a number between 0 and 1 inclusive, where 0 represents an impossible event, 1 represents a certain event, and any number in between represents the relative likelihood of the event occurring. This rule has been stated previously but bears repeating. There cannot be a probability value greater than 1, since nothing can be more certain than certainty. There cannot be a probability value less than 0, since nothing can be less possible than impossibility.

Rule 2. The sum of the probabilities of *all* the states of nature that bear on the consequences of a decision at a specific point in time must equal 1. This simply means that one of the states must occur. If the sum of the state probabilities is less than 1, either some possible state has been ignored or the probabilities assigned to one or more of the identified states are too low. Conversely, if the sum of the state probabilities is greater than 1, one or more of the state probabilities are too high.

Rule 3. For any two mutually exclusive states of nature—say, s_1 and s_2—the probability that either one or the other will occur is simply the sum of the individual probabilities. Remember that the states identified in a decision situation must be mutually exclusive.

Consider the Thompson case first referred to in Chapter 4. Frank Thompson was given the opportunity to purchase anywhere from 0 to 5 building lots from the Tristate Development Company. The states of nature in that case were the possible levels of demand for Thompson's houses on those lots at the price that he would establish. We designated the possible states as s_0 through s_5, where the subscript represented the level of demand. We will consider the methods by which Thompson might arrive at an assessment of the specific probabilities a little later. For the time being we will use this case to illustrate the three probability rules mentioned above.

Suppose that Frank Thompson's initial probability assessments are as follows, where the symbol $P(s)$ represents the probability assigned to a state.

State	$P(s)$
s_0	.10
s_1	.15
s_2	.30
s_3	.25
s_4	.15
s_5	.10
	1.05

Each probability value assigned to a state is a number between 0 and 1, as required by rule 1. However, the sum of all the individual state probabilities is 1.05. This violates rule 2, which specifies that the sum must exactly equal 1. Thompson must therefore reassess the individual probabilities, since at least one of them is too large.

As a second approximation, Thompson arrives at the following set of probabilities:

State	$P(s)$
s_0	.10
s_1	.15
s_2	.25
s_3	.20
s_4	.15
s_5	.10
	.95

Now the sum of the state probabilities is less than 1, which also violates rule 2. Either one or more of the states are assessed too low or there are one or more additional states that have been overlooked. For example, perhaps there should be another state, s_6, which represents the probability of a demand for 6 or more houses. This state might have a probability of .05, which would bring the sum of all the state probabilities to 1.00. However, since Thompson is offered a maximum of 5 lots, this state, s_6, does not have a bearing on his decision situation. Consequently, the individual state probabilities must be reevaluated. Thompson's final set of probabilities is:

State	$P(s)$
s_0	.10
s_1	.20
s_2	.25
s_3	.20
s_4	.15
s_5	.10
	1.00

Now each state probability is between 0 and 1 and the sum is exactly equal to 1. The complete set of probabilities on all the states is called a *probability distribution*.

According to rule 3, the probability of any two states occurring is the sum of their individual probabilities. Thus Thompson should be able to say that the probability that there will be a demand for either 2 or 3 houses is .45 (.25 + .20). The probability that there will be a demand for 2, 3, or 4 houses is .60 (.25 + .20 + .15).

ASSESSING STATE PROBABILITIES

Every decision maker must have some information about the environment in which he must make decisions. If this were not so, it is unlikely that he would have decision-making responsibility. Of course, the amount and type of information he might have will vary from decision situation to decision situation. Sometimes, when the amount of available information is sparse, there is time to acquire additional information. Often, though, the sheer quantity of available information is so great that the decision maker does not have the time to evaluate all of it. In fact, the major constraint imposed on the decision maker is usually not the availability of information but rather the time he has to make the decision.

Even though we have adopted the subjective view of probability, the decision maker should consider empirical evidence when he makes his probability assessments—if only to verify that those assessments are reasonably consistent with the available evidence. However, empirical data are also useful in helping the decision maker arrive at his assessments. For example, suppose we have data which indicate that a particular salesman in our organization was successful in making a sale on 3 out of 10 presentations. Using this evidence, we assess the probability of this salesman's making a sale as 3 out of 10, or 3/10, or simply .3. We should not interpret this to mean that he will make a sale exactly 3 times in every 10 presentations. In fact, he may make only a single sale in the next 10 presentations and then be successful 5 times in the 10 presentations that follow. It would be more accurate to interpret this probability as a long-run average. In fact, if we only had data on as few as 10 sales presentations we might be hesitant about committing ourselves to a probability assessment of exactly .3. On his next presentations he might fail to make even one sale. What would this do to our probability assessment?

On the other hand, if we had data on 100 presentations made by this salesman which resulted in 32 sales, we might conclude that an appropriate probability of making a sale for this salesman would be 32/100, or .32. However, it is quite likely that in a subsequent series of 100 presentations he might actually make fewer than 32 or more than 32 sales. In fact, on the basis of data on the first 100 presentations we might be more comfortable in estimating this probability as .30 or .35. And this brings us to the question of how precise our probability assessments should be.

Most people do not think of probability in terms of a scale of values ranging from 0 to 1. In fact, most people recognize only two distinct probability values: "it probably will" and "it probably won't." If, in considering some uncertain event, they make the assessment that "it probably will" occur, they usually act as though the event were certain to happen—that is, as though it had a probability of 1. If their assessment is "it probably won't," they generally act as though the event were impossible and had a probability of 0. In other words, even when the probability of an event is a consideration in making a decision, most decision makers use only probabilities of 0 and 1 and tend to ignore any values between those two extremes. This, of course, is essentially the same as using the criteria of optimism and pessimism described in Chapter 5. And, in fact, for the decision maker who recognizes only two probability values, those two criteria are sufficient for his needs. Their use will not lead to optimal decisions but will probably result in a good decision about 50% of the time—which appears to be about par for the course.

The slightly more sophisticated decision maker will recognize a third probability value. In addition to "it probably will" and "it probably won't," there is a third point on his probability scale: "it's a toss-up." For a decision situation with only two states of nature, "it's a toss-up" corresponds to a probability of .5. Usually if the decision maker's assessment is "it's a toss-up," he really doesn't know what to do and may even resort to tossing a coin in order to make his decision. In this type of situation he should adopt the criterion of neutrality and act as though all possible states were equally likely to occur. He should then select the act with the highest average payoff where this value corresponds to an unweighted average as described in Chapter 5. Again, he will not be making optimal decisions and his decision-making score will not improve very much, but at least he will have some consistent procedure for making decisions.

A probability scale with values of only 0 and 1 or 0, .5, and 1 is much too coarse for good decision making. By the same token, a scale that requires distinctions as narrow as .01 is overly fine and really isn't necessary for good decision making, though in many instances such fine distinctions are convenient. Few individuals are sensitive to the difference between probability values such as .31 and .32 or .64 and .65. There are very few decision situations in which the consequences would be affected by a 1% change in the probability of a state. In fact, consequences in a decision situation are frequently insensitive to changes of 5%, 10%, or even more in state probabilities. We will consider this question of sensitivity in a later chapter.

Since small differences of a few percentage points in probability assessments will usually have no significant effect in making optimal decisions, the decision maker should be allowed some leeway in deviating from the precise values computed from empirical data. Consequently, if data indicate that a salesman experienced 32 successes in 100 sales presentations we could estimate his success probability as .32. However, for the same data, an estimate of .30 or 1/3 or even .35 would not be unreasonable.

One other point about probability assessments warrants discussion. If the available data relate to the experience of a single salesman, then the estimated probability of making a sale based on these data applies only to that salesman, not to all the other salesmen in the organization—that is, unless we can assume that this particular salesman is representative of the entire sales force. Sometimes such representativeness must be assumed because we have no other data or other basis for making the probability assessment. However, if the data indicating 32 sales out of 100 presentations were a composite of the experience of the entire sales force, this probability would be applicable to the sales force as a whole and might be interpreted as the probability of a presentation made by any salesman resulting in a sale. In basing probability assessments on empirical data, the decision maker must consider the representativeness of the data. In other words, do the data really represent the state or states in the decision situation?

Unfortunately, in most managerial decision situations it is impossible to observe data that truly represent the states involved. The only time this occurs is with repetitive or programmable decisions. Managerial decision situations, at least the tough ones, are usually one-of-a-kind situations and therefore unprogrammable. The best that the manager can do in these situations is to look for similarities between the factors represented by the available data and the states in the decision situation at hand.

Consider, as an example, the bid decision that must be made by Electronic Devices, Inc., first mentioned in Chapter 4. Although EDI has submitted bids for many other government contracts, it has never submitted *this* specific proposal for *this* specific contract. This proposal and this contract are unique. The question is: How representative is EDI's previous record of successful and unsuccessful bids in assessing probabilities in the present decision situation? There is, of course, no clear answer. It is the decision maker who must assess the probabilities, and in that function his judgment is the most important factor.

In the Thompson case, Frank Thompson has purchased land and built and sold similar houses on many previous occasions. But how representative is his past experience in assessing the probability of the demand for these specific houses on these lots at this particular time? Again, only the decision maker can answer that question. He must combine his subjective judgment and knowledge with whatever empirical data he can muster in determining just how representative the data are and how they should be applied to the assessment of state probabilities in the present decision situation. No rules can be established for this procedure. This is where the word "intuitive" assumes significance in the formal intuitive procedure.

PROBABILITY AND ODDS

Everyone is familiar with the concept of odds. Even people who have never placed a bet on anything know, at least in a vague way, what odds represent. If you give 2-to-1 odds on a bet, you must risk 2 units in order to win 1. Therefore, odds are closely related to the stakes or the amount at risk in a betting situation.

Odds are also related to the probability of winning. An event for which the odds are 10 to 1 in favor is a great deal more likely to occur than an event for which the odds are only 2 to 1 in favor, which in turn is a great deal more likely to occur than an event for which the odds are only 1 to 2 in favor. Of course, odds can be stated in favor of an event or against an event. In our discussion, we will always specify odds "for" the event occurring.

Whenever odds are quoted for or against some event, it is usually in the context of betting or gambling. This is probably because it is gamblers who have consistently adopted this measure of likelihood in placing bets and taking bets and making payoffs. The better a gambler is able to assess the actual odds and then make the most favorable bets, the more successful he is likely to be.

Most managers do not consider themselves to be gamblers, even though they must frequently make decisions under similar conditions of uncertainty. Consequently, we seldom hear odds being quoted on the behavior of a particular stock, the price of land, or the availability of some raw material or commodity. Good decision makers, however, do make this type of assessment, either consciously or unconsciously, before choosing among the alternatives in their decision situation—particularly when the results of the decision have monetary consequences.

Odds are a convenient method for assessing probabilities because they are often interpreted and expressed in terms of the dollar amount of the payoff an individual would receive in return for a specified number of dollars bet on an event if that event actually occurs. If the event fails to occur, his payoff would, of course, be negative, that is, a loss. For example, if you made a bet at odds of 3 to 1 and won, your payoff would be $3.00 for each $1.00 you bet. On the other hand, if you bet at odds of 1 to 3 and won, you would receive only $1.00 for every $3.00 you bet. In other words, in order to get someone to take a bet on an event with odds of 1 to 3, you would have to risk $3.00 for the opportunity to win $1.00, while the other person would be risking only $1.00 for the opportunity to win $3.00.

Let's now consider how odds are related to probabilities. A probability, as we have already stated, is a number between 0 and 1 inclusive and therefore can be expressed as a fraction. This can be either a proper fraction such as 7/10 or a decimal fraction such as .7. Any decimal fraction can be converted to a proper fraction and vice versa. If we start with a probability expressed as a decimal fraction such as .7, the first step in converting that value to odds is to state the value as a proper fraction—7/10. A probability stated in this form can also be expressed in words: "The chances of the event occurring are 7 out of 10." Now, if an event has 7 chances in 10 of occurring, it must have 3 chances in 10 of not occurring. Consequently, the odds in favor of the event are 7 to 3.

The odds for an event are expressed as the ratio of two numbers which represent the number of chances in favor of the event to the number of chances against. Since we have adopted the subjective viewpoint of probability, the odds or odds ratios are also considered from the decision maker's subjective viewpoint.

For many decision makers, it is easier to make a subjective assessment of odds than it is to express probabilities directly. Once the decision maker has established subjective odds for the event (such as 7 to 3), the probability, expressed as a fraction, can be determined very easily. This is done by constructing a proper fraction with the two numbers in the odds ratio added together and placed in the denominator. The single number which refers to the chances of the event occurring is placed in the numerator. That is:

$$\text{Probability} = \frac{\text{chances in favor}}{\text{chances in favor} + \text{chances against}}$$

In the case of odds of 7 to 3, the corresponding probability is:

$$\frac{7}{7+3} = \frac{7}{10} = .7$$

Now, how is the decision maker to determine whether he believes that the odds in favor of an event are 3 to 2 or 7 to 3 or 60 to 40? The best method for assessing odds, particularly in a nonprogrammable, one-of-a-kind decision situation, is to relate them to the monetary risk one would be willing to assume in betting on the event.

For example, next season the Los Angeles Rams will play the Minnesota Vikings only once. If the odds favor the Rams by 2 to 1, what does that actually mean? First, it means that if the odds are assessed correctly it would be reasonable to risk $2.00 by betting on the Rams in order to win $1.00 from someone betting on the Vikings. Or, turning it around, it would be reasonable to risk $1.00 by betting on the Vikings for a chance to win $2.00 from someone betting on the Rams. In another interpretation, these odds express the relative likelihood of either team winning the game. On the basis of the odds, the Rams are twice as likely to win as the Vikings. Or, conversely, the Vikings are half as likely to win as the Rams. If the Rams are twice as likely to win as the Vikings, the chances of the Rams winning are 2 out of 3 and the probability that the Rams will win is:

$$\frac{2}{2+1} = \frac{2}{3} = .67$$

In gambling or in managerial decision situations, the decision maker's assessment of these probabilities is the amount that he would be willing to risk by acting on the assumption that an uncertain event will occur in conjunction with the potential gains or losses that might result.

In the formal intuitive procedure, odds are not as convenient to work with as probabilities. Therefore, whenever you assess likelihoods in terms of odds, you should convert them into probabilities expressed as a decimal fraction. Remember, probabilities represent the likelihood that an event or state will occur and therefore correspond to odds "for" the event.

For the decision maker, assessing probabilities by first attempting to determine odds is a good approach. It is frequently much easier to determine the amount of money you would be willing to risk on an uncertain event in exchange for an opportunity to gain another sum of money than it is to assess the probability of that uncertain event directly. Consider a wager you might make on the outcome of a prizefight. You are betting on fighter B to win over fighter A. If you would be willing to bet $1.00 in order to win $1.00, your assessment of the odds for fighter B are 1 to 1. In other words, you believe that the probability that B will win is:

$$\frac{1}{1+1} = \frac{1}{2} = .50$$

On the other hand, if you would refuse to bet at even money and would be willing to bet your $1.00 only if you could win $2.00, you believe that the odds for fighter B are 1 to 2. In that case, your estimate of the probability of B winning the fight is:

$$\frac{1}{1+2} = \frac{1}{3} = .33$$

If you were quite certain about B's ability and would be willing to bet $2.00 in order to win $1.00, then your assessment of the odds for fighter B would be 2 to 1 and the corresponding probability would be:

$$\frac{2}{2+1} = \frac{2}{3} = .67$$

The process you go through to arrive at a set of betting odds that represent your probability estimates is difficult to explain, since it is highly intuitive. You probably base your assessment on what you know or believe you know about the two fighters. Your knowledge probably results from what you have read or observed about their experience, their previous records, and their physical abilities. Basically, you arrive at a subjective assessment through a conscious and subconscious mental evaluation of all the information you have accumulated about this particular event. The more information you have accumulated, the better your assessment of the odds is likely to be.

Remember that a list of the possible states of nature together with the probability of each state occurring is called a *probability distribution*. A probability distribution is a convenient device for indicating how probabilities are distributed over all the possible states that might occur in a decision situation. Remember, also, that the sum of the probabilities of all the states must equal 1.

In any decision situation involving only two possible states, the decision maker need only determine the odds in favor of one of the states. Once the odds for one state are determined, the odds for the other state are automatically fixed. That is, if there are only two states—call them state A and state B—the odds for A are the same as the odds against B and vice versa. For example, if the odds are 3 to 1 for A, then the odds must be 1 to 3 for B. The respective probabilities of the two states must be 3/4 and 1/4, or .75 and .25.

When there are more than two states in the decision situation, the procedure becomes more complicated. The odds for each possible state should be assessed separately and converted to probabilities, and the probabilities should then be adjusted so that their sum equals 1.

Consider the land purchase decision in the Thompson case. Frank Thompson must assess the probabilities of six different states which correspond to the level of demand for houses that he might build on the lots offered to him for purchase. The possible levels of demand pertinent to his decision situation vary from 0 to 5. Remember that even though Thompson has built and offered similar houses for sale before, he has never attempted to sell these exact houses on these exact lots. This situation and the conditions that affect it are unique. They have never existed in exactly the same way before and will never exist in exactly the same way again. With this in mind, how should Frank Thompson assign probabilities to the states of nature?

The best approach for the decision maker in situations like these is to use all available information in assessing the odds at which he would be willing to risk his capital and then convert those odds to probabilities. Thus Thompson should use all the objective information he can accumulate about the sale of similar properties and whatever subjective information he already has about the real estate market in his area at this time.

Since there are six possible states that will affect the payoffs in the decision problem, Thompson should first consider whether he believes that all these states are equally likely. The states are the sale of 0, 1, 2, 3, 4, or 5 houses. If he does believe that these events are equally likely, he should assign a probability of 1/6 to each event.

Suppose, however, that on further consideration Thompson concludes that some of these events are more likely to occur than others. Since he does not feel he can assign probability numbers directly to each of the six possibilities, he decides to apply the betting-odds procedure to each event and then convert to probabilities later.

First, consider the event that he will sell none of the houses. This may seem to be a very unlikely state. Thompson asks himself at what odds he would be willing to bet that this event will occur. He decides that he would be virtually unwilling to bet on this event at any odds. In other words, he is virtually certain he will sell at least one house. In that case he feels that the event s_0: "sell no houses" is practically impossible. Since impossible events have a probability of 0, he would assign a 0 to the probability of event s_0.

Next, he might consider the possibility that he will sell all the houses—that is, event s_5. Although he believes that this event is not very likely, he doesn't consider it to be impossible. In fact, he would be willing to bet $1.00 on s_5 occurring if he could find someone who would be willing to bet $8.00 that it will not occur. In this case, the odds for s_5 occurring are 1 to 8 and the probability assigned to s_5 is $\frac{1}{1+8} = \frac{1}{9}$.

Now consider each of the other events in turn. Thompson feels practically certain that he will be able to sell at least one house. In fact, he believes it quite likely that he will sell more than one house, and that the sale of *only* one house, though possible, is unlikely. In order to bet $1.00 that he will sell only one house, he would require someone to put up $9.00. Therefore, his odds on the event s_1 are 1 to 9 and the probability assigned to event s_1 is $\frac{1}{1+9} = \frac{1}{10}$.

The most likely event to occur, he believes, is the sale of three houses. He feels strongly enough that he would be willing to bet $4.00 on this event against someone else's $1.00. In other words, he would be willing to risk $4.00 in order to win only

$1.00. The odds for s_3 are therefore 4 to 1 and the corresponding probability is $\dfrac{4}{4+1} = \dfrac{4}{5}$.

The only other events left are s_2 and s_4, the sale of two and four houses respectively. Thompson determines that he would bet on s_2 at odds of 3 to 2 and on s_4 at odds of 2 to 3. The corresponding probabilities are

$$\frac{3}{3+2} = \frac{3}{5} \quad \text{and} \quad \frac{2}{2+3} = \frac{2}{5}$$

Summarizing the assessments thus far, we have:

s_0	s_1	s_2	s_3	s_4	s_5
0	1/10	3/5	4/5	2/5	1/9

Since the sum of the probabilities of *all* possible events must equal 1, we'll have to add these probabilities and see what their total is. To do so, of course, we will first have to find their lowest common denominator—that is, the smallest number that can be evenly divided by all the denominators in the set of fractions. In this case, the lowest common denominator is 90, the smallest number that can be evenly divided by 5, 9, and 10. The equivalent fractions with the same denominator are easily obtained by dividing the denominator of each of the fractions into the lowest common denominator and then multiplying the numerator of that fraction by the result of this division. The answer is then placed over the lowest common denominator.

Converting the original fractions to equivalent fractions with a denominator of 90, we get:

s_0	s_1	s_2	s_3	s_4	s_5
0	9/90	54/90	72/90	36/90	10/90

The sum of all the probability fractions is 181/90. Since such a sum represents a certain event, it should equal 1. Obviously, the sum of our assessed probabilities is considerably greater. We must therefore adjust them so that they do add up to 1. This is accomplished by multiplying each fraction by the reciprocal of the sum. The reciprocal of a fraction is obtained by reversing the numerator and the denominator. The reciprocal of 181/90 is 90/181. Carrying out this operation and then converting each fraction to a decimal, we obtain the following probability distribution for these events:

$$
\begin{array}{llll}
P(s_0): & 0 \times 90/181 = & 0 & = 0 \\
P(s_1): & 9/90 \times 90/181 = & 9/181 & = .05 \\
P(s_2): & 54/90 \times 90/181 = & 54/181 & = .30 \\
P(s_3): & 72/90 \times 90/181 = & 72/181 & = .40 \\
P(s_4): & 36/90 \times 90/181 = & 36/181 & = .20 \\
P(s_5): & 10/90 \times 90/181 = & \underline{10/181} & = \underline{.05} \\
& & 181/181 & 1.00
\end{array}
$$

Thompson's feelings about the likelihood of the six possible states have now been converted into a probability distribution. The sum of all the individual probabilities, each of which is expressed as a decimal, is equal to 1, as it should be. Note that the probabilities here have been rounded to two decimal places. It is quite unlikely that any decision situation would necessitate probabilities expressed to three decimal places. Such extreme precision in expressing probabilities is inconsistent with the subjective nature of the assessments, and the consequences of most decisions are insensitive to small differentials in state probabilities.

SUMMARY OF RULES FOR ASSIGNING PROBABILITIES

A summary of the rules for assigning probability numbers to a set of events follows.

1. If in a given decision situation you have listed a set of n possible mutually exclusive states, and if you are reasonably certain that all the states are equally likely to occur, you should assign a probability of $1/n$ to each event. Convert these proper fractions to decimals by dividing the numerator of the fraction by the denominator.

2. If the states do not seem to be equally likely, use whatever empirical information you have about similar states and similar conditions together with your own subjective information to establish a set of betting odds for each state that is consistent with your feelings.

Remember that the probability numbers you will eventually use should correspond to the probability of the event occurring and therefore are directly related to the odds *for* or *in favor of* the event. If you can decide on the number of dollars that you would be willing to risk in betting that the event will occur and the number of dollars of payoff that you would require an opponent to risk, you can determine the odds *for* the event, expressed as a ratio of your dollars to your opponent's dollars. To convert these odds to a probability number, use the following formula:

$$\frac{\text{Number of your dollars}}{\text{Number of your dollars + number of your opponent's dollars}}$$

Convert this fraction to a decimal by dividing the numerator by the denominator. This is the probability of the event occurring.

3. The sum of all the probability numbers for all possible events must equal 1. (Minor discrepancies due to rounding individual numbers are not important.) When a set of events is evaluated in terms of odds *for* and is then converted to probabilities, it is quite likely that their sum will not equal 1. When this occurs, the individual values must be adjusted as follows:

First, using the probabilities expressed as proper fractions, find the lowest common denominator for all the fractions and express each fraction in terms of the common denominator. Second, add all the fractions. If this sum is not equal to 1, determine a *correction factor*. This correction factor is obtained by inverting the fraction you obtained as the sum. That is, the previous numerator becomes the denominator of your correction factor and the previous denominator becomes its numerator.

Third, multiply each probability fraction by the correction factor. The new set of fractions should add up to 1. Finally, convert each new probability fraction to a decimal. The decimals should also add up to 1 or approximately so. This set of decimals represents your final probabilities for all the possible events—in other words, your probability distribution.

NORMAL PROBABILITIES

When several states of nature must be considered in a decision situation, it is often difficult to assess each state probability individually. The more states there are, the more difficult this becomes. In such a case, a very common probability distribution, called the *normal distribution,* can be used as a model for the state probabilities. This distribution is easier for the decision maker to use, since it requires fewer individual assessments.

In order for this approach to be effective, the decision situation must have certain characteristics. First, the states of nature must be values on some numerical scale. That is, each state must be represented by a number that is part of a logical sequence of numbers representing the other states. The normal distribution would not apply when the states are qualitative attributes such as "good," "moderate," and "poor," or "gets contract" and "doesn't get contract." It would apply, however, in the Thompson case, where the states (demand for houses) are represented by the numbers 0 through 5, and in the Eastways case, where the states (product sales) are numbers from 2,000 through 8,000.

Second, the normal distribution is applicable only to situations involving multiple states, and as a rule of thumb we will say that there should be at least five states of nature. When there are fewer than five states, individual probability assessments do not create an insurmountable problem. Finally, it should be reasonable for the decision maker to assume that there is some average or most likely value of the states and that the individual state probabilities decline symmetrically on both sides of that average, which we will designate M. In other words, the probability distribution should look approximately like the bell-shaped curve in Figure 7.1.

The bell-shaped curve can be used as a model for many physical phenomena. Most sets of physical measurements tend to cluster about an average or mean value and decline in frequency as deviations from the mean in both directions increase. However, not only is the normal distribution a model for the distribution of the frequencies of values, it is also a model for the distribution of the probabilities of these values occurring. The area under the curve between any two values on the horizontal scale represents the probability of occurrence of a value in that region. Consequently, this model is extremely useful in helping the decision maker assign probabilities to the set of states without requiring him to assess each state probability individu-

FIGURE 7.1 Normal probability distribution.

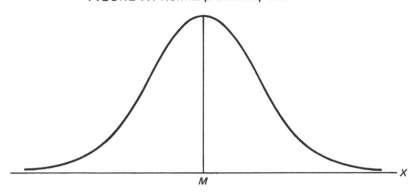

ally. However, this does not relieve the decision maker of his judgmental responsibilities, since there are still two very important assessments he must make. First, he must estimate an average or mean value of the numerical states; second, he must express his uncertainty about this mean value with another measure, which we will call the standard deviation.

Before we apply the normal distribution to the problem of assessing state probabilities, let's examine once more some of the characteristics of this very useful tool. If X represents the numerical values that the various states could assume and M is the mean or most likely value, the curve declines *symmetrically* on both sides of the mean. That is, both halves of the curve are identical. The probability that the value of X falls between any two points on the horizontal axis is represented by the area under the curve between those two points. The total area under the curve is equivalent to a probability of 1, and the area on each side of the mean represents a probability of .5.

All normal distributions do not look exactly alike. Although they all resemble the curve shown in Figure 7.1, some are relatively narrow—that is, the curve is concentrated close to the mean—while others are wider and more spread out from the mean. Figure 7.2 illustrates two normal distributions that have the same mean value but differ considerably in variability. We will measure this variability about the mean with the standard deviation, which we will designate S and which will represent a

FIGURE 7.2 Two normal distributions.

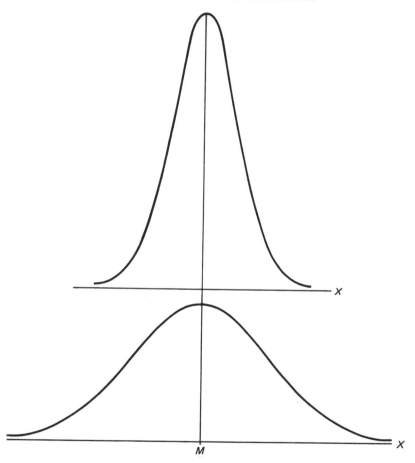

measure of the decision maker's uncertainty about his estimate of the mean.

Once values have been determined for M and S, it is possible to use a simple table to determine the probability that the state value X will fall in any region whatsoever. In order to use this table, we must first convert the value of X to another value called a Z score. This is a very simple matter and is accomplished with the following formula:

$$Z = \frac{X - M}{S}$$

To find the normal probabilities, we refer to Table 7.1, the table of the standard normal distribution. The standard normal distribution is a normal distribution with the mean equal to 0 and the standard deviation equal to 1. To find probabilities for any value of X which has a normal distribution and for which M and S are specified, we convert to a Z score and determine the appropriate probability from the table. Note that the table provides the probability that the state has a value *less than or equal to* Z. This probability corresponds to the shaded area in the diagram.

TABLE 7.1 Table of areas for the standard normal probability distribution.

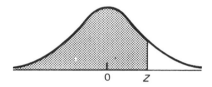

Z	Area to Left of Z	Z	Area to Left of Z
.0	.5000	2.0	.9772
.1	.5398	2.1	.9821
.2	.5793	2.2	.9861
.3	.6179	2.3	.9893
.4	.6554	2.4	.9918
.5	.6915	2.5	.9938
.6	.7257	2.6	.9953
.7	.7580	2.7	.9965
.8	.7881	2.8	.9974
.9	.8159	2.9	.9981
1.0	.8413	3.0	.9987
1.1	.8643	3.1	.9990
1.2	.8849	3.2	.9993
1.3	.9032	3.3	.9995
1.4	.9192	3.4	.9997
1.5	.9332	3.5	.9998
1.6	.9452	3.6	.9998
1.7	.9554	3.7	.9999
1.8	.9641	3.8	.9999
1.9	.9713	3.9	.9999
		4.0	1.000

For example, suppose that we want to determine the probability that the state represented by X has a value less than or equal to 130. We assume that the distribution of X is normal, with $M = 100$ and $S = 15$. The first step is to find a Z score that corresponds to $X = 100$. This is obtained as follows:

$$Z = \frac{X - M}{S} = \frac{130 - 100}{15} = 2$$

Therefore, the probability that X is less than or equal to 130 is the same as the probability that Z is less than or equal to 2. This probability can be read from Table 7.1 as .9772.

To find the probability that X is greater than 130, we simply find the probability that Z is greater than 2. This corresponds to the unshaded area in the right-hand tail of the diagram (Table 7.1). Since the total area under the curve is equivalent to a probability of 1, the area to the right of Z must be equal to 1 minus the area to the left of Z. Therefore, the desired probability is $1 - .9772 = .0228$.

Although it may not be immediately apparent, Z is the distance between the mean of the distribution and the specified value of X measured in units of the standard deviation. The value $Z = 2$ means that the value of X (in this case, 130) is two standard deviations above the mean of the distribution. Similarly, $Z = -2$ represents a value of X two standard deviations below the mean. For example, if X is distributed normally with $M = 100$ and $S = 15$, Figure 7.3 shows that distribution with various values of X and the corresponding value of Z. It also shows the percentage of the area that falls within the interval defined by the mean plus and minus one, two, and three standard deviations for any normal distribution.

Since the normal distribution is symmetrical and the total area under the curve is equal to 1, the area on each side of the mean must be equal to .5. Also, if the area between $Z = -1$ and $Z = +1$ is equal to .6826, then the area from the mean out to either $Z = -1$ or $Z = +1$ is equal to .3413.

The table of the standard normal distribution provides areas or probabilities for values from $Z = 0$ to $Z = 4$. Probabilities are provided only for positive values of Z. Because of the symmetry of the distribution, all areas below the mean which correspond to

FIGURE 7.3 Normal distribution of *X* and *Z*.

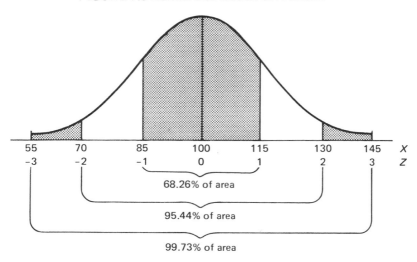

negative values of *Z* are identical to the corresponding areas above the mean. A more extensive table of normal probabilities is provided in the appendix.

One further example may be helpful. To find the probability that *X* falls between 130 and 115, we must convert both values to *Z* scores. We already know that *X* = 130 corresponds to *Z* = 2. The *Z* score corresponding to *X* = 115 is:

$$Z = \frac{X - M}{X} = \frac{115 - 100}{15} = 1$$

The probability that *X* lies between 115 and 130 is equivalent to the probability that *Z* lies between 1 and 2. This is obtained by subtracting the probability that *Z* is less than or equal to 1 from the probability that *Z* is less than or equal to 2. That is, .9772 − .8413 = .1359. The probability or area between any two points on the horizontal scale can be obtained in the same way.

Once you have converted any value of *X* to a corresponding value of *Z* and determined the appropriate probabilities from the table, you can associate these probabilities with the specific values of the states in the decision situation. We will illustrate the entire procedure with reference to the Eastways case.

The Eastways Case

In the Eastways decision situation, the states of nature were various levels of sales of a new product. These levels were stated in increments of 1,000 units, as follows:

$$s_1: \quad 2,000 \text{ units}$$
$$s_2: \quad 3,000 \text{ units}$$
$$s_3: \quad 4,000 \text{ units}$$
$$s_4: \quad 5,000 \text{ units}$$
$$s_5: \quad 6,000 \text{ units}$$
$$s_6: \quad 7,000 \text{ units}$$
$$s_7: \quad 8,000 \text{ units}$$

It is important to realize that the selection of 1,000-unit increments was a matter of judgment and convenience. Too many small increments would result in a multitude of states and would simply complicate the analysis. On the other hand, too few large increments would fail to discriminate sufficiently among the possibilities and their effects on the consequences of the decision. However, it should be obvious that the actual sales could differ by increments of 1 unit and the states could conceivably have values like 2,354 units and 4,179 units. Therefore, state s_1 (2,000 units) actually includes sales of between 1,500 and 2,500 units. State s_2 (3,000) units represents sales of between 2,500 and 3,500 units, and so on. If we were to draw a diagram of these states and an approximating normal distribution, it would look like Figure 7.4. With this approximation, the probability assigned to state s_1 actually corresponds to the area between 1,500 and 2,500. The probability assigned to s_2 corresponds to the area between 2,500 and 3,500, and so on. Since the area under the curve tends to disappear below 1,500 and above 8,500, we can for practical purposes ignore values beyond those limits.

Our goal now is to determine the normal probabilities that correspond to each state represented by a distinct area under the curve. Since all areas under a normal probability distribution can be determined if the values of the mean and standard deviation are known, the decision maker's first task is to assess his subjective values of M and S. It is, of course, much easier to estimate these two values than it is to estimate odds or probabilities for each of the seven possible states. We will illustrate how these assessments should be made in the next section.

For the time being, we will assume that the estimates have been made in the Eastways case and the decision maker has determined subjectively that $M = 5,000$ and $S = 1,000$. The procedure for assigning probabilities to the states is as follows:

1. Convert the numerical value of X at the *upper* limit of each area which represents a state to a Z score and round off that value to tenths—that is, to one place to the right of the decimal point.
2. Determine from Table 7.1 the proportion of the area under the curve that lies below, or to the left of, the Z score for each value of Z computed above.
3. Subtract each of these proportions or probabilities from the next higher proportion. The remainder represents the proportion of the area in each curve segment—that is, the probability of each state.

The procedure for the Eastways case is described below. Figure 7.4 shows the normal distribution with the Z scores indicated.

Step 1.	X Upper Limit	$\dfrac{X - M}{S}$		Z
	8,500	$\dfrac{8,500 - 5,000}{1,000}$	=	3.5
	7,500	$\dfrac{7,500 - 5,000}{1,000}$	=	2.5
	6,500	$\dfrac{6,500 - 5,000}{1,000}$	=	1.5
	5,500	$\dfrac{5,500 - 5,000}{1,000}$	=	.5
	4,500	$\dfrac{4,500 - 5,000}{1,000}$	=	$-$ .5
	3,500	$\dfrac{3,500 - 5,000}{1,000}$	=	$-$ 1.5
	2,500	$\dfrac{2,500 - 5,000}{1,000}$	=	$-$ 2.5

Step 2.

Z Score	Area to Left of Z	Obtained
3.5	.9998	directly from Table 7.1
2.5	.9938	directly from table
1.5	.9332	directly from table
.5	.6915	directly from table
− .5	.3085	1 − .6915 = .3085
−1.5	.0668	1 − .9332 = .0668
−2.5	.0062	1 − .9938 = .0062

Step 3.

State	Area or Probability Corresponding to Each State	Rounded Probability
s_7: 8,000	.9998 − .9938 = .0060	.01
s_6: 7,000	.9938 − .9332 = .0604	.06
s_5: 6,000	.9332 − .6915 = .2417	.24
s_4: 5,000	.6915 − .3085 = .3830	.38
s_3: 4,000	.3085 − .0668 = .2417	.24
s_2: 3,000	.0668 − .0062 = .0606	.06
s_1: 2,000	.0062 − 0 = .0062	.01
		1.00

FIGURE 7.4 Normal approximation to the states in the Eastways case, showing Z scores.

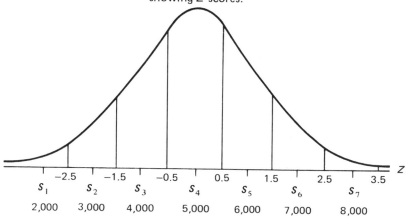

ASSESSING THE MEAN AND STANDARD DEVIATION OF A NORMAL PROBABILITY DISTRIBUTION

To illustrate the subjective assessment of the mean and standard deviation of a normal probability distribution, we will return to the concept of betting odds. However, we will use the concept of odds somewhat differently than we did in assessing state probabilities directly. Let's begin with a procedure for estimating the mean, which is sometimes called the *expected value*. This term is helpful because it allows the decision maker to think of the mean as the value he would most expect to occur—in other words, a most likely value.

Look once again at a normal probability distribution, as shown in Figure 7.5. Fifty percent of the area under the curve lies on each side of the mean or expected value. Since area represents probability, the probability of obtaining a value below the mean is equal to the probability of obtaining a value above the mean, and both of these probabilities are .5. In terms of odds, the odds on both of these events are even, or 1 to 1.

In assessing the mean or expected value of his subjective probability distribution on the possible states of nature, the decision maker should ask himself the following question: "If I had to risk a significant amount of money at even odds that the value of the state most likely to occur is either greater than M or less than M, what should the value of M be in order for me to be willing to take either side of the bet?" The decision maker may not arrive at his final estimate of M immediately. In fact, he may have to make several adjustments to his initial estimate.

Suppose, for example, that the president of Eastways, the decision maker in the case, initially estimated the mean number

FIGURE 7.5 Normal probability distribution.

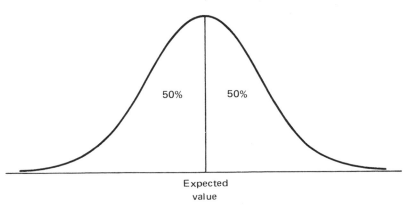

Expected
value

of units he believed would be sold as 4,000. If 4,000 is his true subjective mean, he would have to believe that sales of fewer than 4,000 units are just as likely as sales of more than 4,000 units. Therefore, he should be willing to bet on either side of that proposition at even odds. If after initially selecting 4,000 as his mean, he would not be willing to take either side of the bet at even odds, then his true subjective mean is not 4,000 and that value must be adjusted either upward or downward.

Suppose that after considering both sides of the stated wager, the president of Eastways decides that he would prefer to bet that sales will be greater than 4,000 rather than less. In that case, his mean should be adjusted upward. Suppose his next estimate of the mean is 5,000 and he once again considers how he feels about the two sides of the wager. This time, he would prefer to bet that sales will be less than 5,000 units than bet that they will be greater than 5,000. In this case, his estimated mean is too high and should be adjusted downward. Since 4,000 was too low and 5,000 is too high, he might try 4,500 units as the mean and consider the same bet. If he is indifferent to which side of the wager he takes when the mean is set at 4,500, then this represents his subjective mean of the state probability distribution. Notice that the mean or expected value does not have to be, and in this sense is not, one of the values originally chosen to represent the states. In other words, s_3 was represented by the number 4,000 and s_4 was represented by the number 5,000. The mean is neither of these values.

In most decision situations, it is fairly easy to estimate the mean. The estimate of the standard deviation is somewhat more difficult. Once the mean or expected value is established, the decision maker should pick two additional numbers. These two numbers should be on either side of the mean and equally distant from it. We will call the lower value L and the upper value U. These values should be selected on the basis of the following question: "If I had to risk a significant amount of money at even odds that the value of the state most likely to occur either lies between L and U or does not lie between L and U, what should the values of L and U be in order for me to be completely indifferent as to which side of the wager I would take?"

Once M has been determined, the choice of values for L and U should divide the normal distribution into three parts. Thus, in Figure 7.6, lines through the distribution at L and U divide the curve in such a way that the shaded area of the two tails is exactly equal to the unshaded area in the center. This means that the probabilities associated with both sides of the wager are equal and the odds are even. The distance between L and M and between M and U is equal to d. Or, more simply:

$$d = \frac{U - L}{2}$$

Once the decision maker has determined the values of L and U, the standard deviation of his subjective probability distribution is easily determined from:

$$S = \frac{d}{.675}$$

This formula is derived from the relationship of any deviation from the mean of a normal distribution to the corresponding area under the curve. It is sufficient to state here that lines drawn through the distribution at distances of .675 standard deviations above and below the mean divide the area under the curve as shown in Figure 7.6.

With values for the mean and standard deviation of his subjective normal probability distribution established, the decision

FIGURE 7.6 Normal distribution divided so that the two tail areas combined equal the central areas.

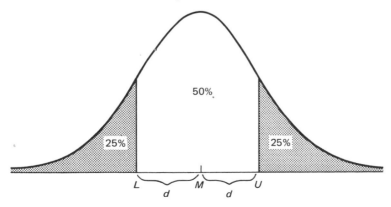

maker can now determine the probability of each state of nature by using the procedure described in the previous section. Again we will illustrate the entire procedure with reference to the Eastways case.

Back to the Eastways Case

The president of Eastways is having difficulty assigning probabilities to the states in his decision situation. He is discussing this problem with his executive vice president and their conversation proceeds as follows:

PRES: My best estimate is that sales could be anywhere from 2,000 to 8,000 units, but I'm having difficulty assessing probabilities for each individual level of sales.

E.V.P.: We could use a normal probability distribution to represent those probabilities. But even if we do that, there are a couple of estimates you must make.

PRES: Okay, let's try that. How do we get started?

E.V.P.: First you must understand that the normal distribution is symmetrical. This means that there is some mean or most likely value of sales, and the probability that actual sales will exceed that value is exactly equal to the probability that sales will be less than that value. If that seems to be a reasonable assumption to you, then the first step is to estimate what you think the most likely value is.

PRES: Well, if I am correct in believing that sales could be anywhere from 2,000 to 8000 units, we could pick the middle value, 5,000. Is that what you mean?

E.V.P.: Not necessarily. The value 5,000 could be your best estimate of the mean, but it is based on your previous estimate of a highest and lowest value. Suppose that there is a possibility that sales could be less than 2,000 or greater than 8,000. Then 5,000 would not necessarily be the middle value. We should try to estimate the mean independently of your estimates of high and low values. However, 5,000 might be a good starting point.

PRES: All right, then. Let's assume, at least for now, that my best estimate of the most likely level of sales is 5,000 units.

E.V.P.: Fine. Now let's see if you would be willing to bet on it. Think of a wager of $1,000 at even money. You can bet either that actual sales will be less than 5,000 units or that actual sales will be more than 5,000 units. Which side of the bet would you rather take?

PRES: Well, if I had to make a choice, I'd probably prefer to bet that sales would be less than 5,000 units.

E.V.P.: Would you be willing to bet on the other side—that is, that sales would be greater than 5,000?

PRES: Well, with $1,000 at stake I'd prefer to bet that sales would be less than 5,000. If I had to take the other side, I guess I'd want more favorable odds.

E.V.P.: If that's how you really feel, then the mean of your probability distribution is not 5,000. It is, in fact, something less than that. Think about 4,000 for a minute. Would you have a preference for betting on one side or the other if the number was 4,000?

PRES: In that case, I'd prefer to bet that sales would be greater than 4,000 units.

E.V.P.: If you are sure about your answers to both of my questions, then your subjective mean lies somewhere between 4,000 and 5,000. How would you bet if the number was 4,500?

PRES: That's a tough one. If that were the bet, I guess I'd be indifferent to which side I took. I guess I'd be willing to bet either way.

E.V.P.: If that's the way you feel, then your subjective estimate of the mean of the distribution of sales is 4,500.

Two people, using this type of question-and-answer technique, can often obtain the appropriate estimates quicker and more easily than the decision maker alone. The decision maker can concentrate entirely on his subjective information while someone else concentrates on the questions to be asked.

The conversation between the president and the executive vice president continues.

E.V.P.: Now that we have the mean, we have to get you to estimate the standard deviation of the distribution. I want to ask you to pick two numbers, which we'll call U and L.

U will be some distance above your mean and L will be the same distance below it. Choose these numbers so that if you had to make an even-money bet of $1,000 that sales would be between U and L or that they would not, you would be willing to bet either way.

PRES: This is a little harder to visualize, but for starters I'll try 3,500 for L and 5,500 for U. Each is a distance of 1,000 units from the mean.

E.V.P.: Okay. Now remember the $1,000 wager. You can bet either that sales will be between 3,500 and 5,500 units or you can bet that they won't. Which side would you prefer to bet on?

PRES: Well, frankly, I'd prefer to bet that actual sales would fall somewhere between 3,500 and 5,500 units than that they would be either less than 3,500 or more than 5,500.

E.V.P.: Since you have a preference, let's narrow the interval. Suppose that L was 4,000 and U was 5,000. Now which side would you prefer to bet on?

PRES: That's a pretty narrow interval. I'd be reluctant to risk $1,000 at even money on that interval. I guess I'd prefer to bet that actual sales would not be in that interval.

E.V.P.: Let's try 3,750 and 5,250 for L and U. Now which side would you bet on?

PRES: In that case, I'd be willing to bet either way.

E.V.P.: Fine. Now we can determine the standard deviation of your distribution:

$$\frac{U - L}{2} = \frac{5,250 - 3,750}{2} = \frac{1,500}{2} = 750 = d$$

Therefore: $S = \dfrac{d}{.675} = \dfrac{750}{.675} = 1,111$

To keep things simple, let's round that off to 1,100 and say the mean and the standard deviation of your distribution are $M = 4,500$ and $S = 1,100$.

Once the mean and the standard deviation have been determined, the normal probabilities for the states can be obtained through the procedure illustrated previously. A picture of the distribution with 4,500 as the mean is provided in Figure 7.7.

FIGURE 7.7 Normal probability distribution on the states
in the Eastway case.

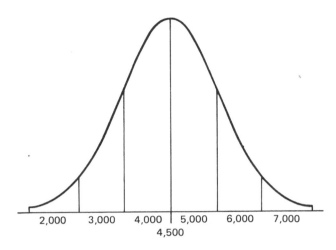

2,000   3,000   4,000 | 5,000   6,000   7,000
                      4,500

The procedure for assigning probabilities to the states follows:

Step 1.

X Upper Limit	$\dfrac{X - M}{S}$	Z
8,500	$\dfrac{8,500 - 4,500}{1,100} =$	3.6
7,500	$\dfrac{7,500 - 4,500}{1,100} =$	2.7
6,500	$\dfrac{6,500 - 4,500}{1,100} =$	1.8
5,500	$\dfrac{5,500 - 4,500}{1,100} =$	.9
4,500	$\dfrac{4,500 - 4,500}{1,100} =$	0
3,500	$\dfrac{3,500 - 4,500}{1,100} =$	−.9
2,500	$\dfrac{2,500 - 4,500}{1,100} =$	−1.8
1,500	$\dfrac{1,500 - 4,500}{1,100} =$	−2.7

Step 2.

Z Score	Area to Left of Z	Obtained
3.6	.9998	directly from Table 7.1
2.7	.9965	directly from table
1.8	.9641	directly from table
.9	.8159	directly from table
0	.5000	directly from table
− .9	.1841	$1 - .8159 = .1841$
−1.8	.0359	$1 - .9641 = .0359$
−2.7	.0035	$1 - .9965 = .0035$

Step 3.

State	Area or Probability Corresponding to Each State	Rounded Probability
s_7: 8,000	$.9998 - .9965 = .0033$	0
s_6: 7,000	$.9965 - .9641 = .0324$	.03
s_5: 6,000	$.9641 - .8159 = .1482$	.15
s_4: 5,000	$.8159 - .5000 = .3159$	.32
s_3: 4,000	$.5000 - .1841 = .3159$	.32
s_2: 3,000	$.1841 - .0359 - .1482$	.15
s_1: 2,000	$.0359 - .0035 = .0324$	.03
s_0: 1,000	$.0035 - 0 = .0035$	0

Since the probabilities assigned to states s_7 and s_0 are 0, these states can be eliminated. The final listing of states and probabilities for this decision situation are:

State	Probability
s_6: 7,000	.03
s_5: 6,000	.15
s_4: 5,000	.32
s_3: 4,000	.32
s_2: 3,000	.15
s_1: 2,000	.03
	1.00

RECAPITULATING PROBABILITY

This chapter on probability has been a lengthy one. It is, however, one of the most important chapters in the book, since the concept of probability as a measurement of uncertainty is the cornerstone of formal intuitive decision making.

In practical decision situations, the final probability distribution on the states of nature usually results from a series of successive approximations, as does the final problem description in a payoff table or a decision tree. The greater the number of pertinent states to which probabilities must be assigned, the greater the number of approximations the decision maker must make before arriving at the set of probabilities that best represent his true subjective assessments.

This chapter has provided two methods for estimating probabilities. The first method assesses probabilities in terms of odds for each of the states separately. These odds are converted to probabilities and then adjusted in order to meet the requirements of a probability distribution. When there are five or more numerically valued states in the problem, another method can be used. This second method utilizes the normal probability distribution as a model for the state probabilities and requires that the decision maker estimate only the mean and standard deviation of the distribution. Once these two values have been established, the probabilities for the individual states can be determined as illustrated.

In appropriate decision situations, both methods can be used to obtain state probabilities, and the differences resulting from each method can then be reconciled by the decision maker. The important thing is that the state probability distribution finally adopted be truly representative of the decision maker's subjective feelings. When the decision maker can honestly say that the probability distribution is consistent with his subjective judgment, he can make his decision using the formal intuitive method.

8

THE USE OF DATA

A decision maker uses data as a source of information about the factors that affect his decision situation. However, data exist in many different forms. There are, of course, subjective data—the information stored in the mind of the decision maker. We have already discussed subjective data, their origin, validity, and use. There are also objective or empirical data, which result from experimentation or simply from the observation and recording of events as they occur. In most decision situations, the decision maker does not have the time to design and conduct an experiment in order to obtain information about his problem. When such an experiment is possible, the resulting information is valuable and should certainly be used. In most cases, however, the decision maker must rely on already existing data, which have not necessarily been collected for the express purpose of providing information about his decision situation. Nevertheless, such data should be evaluated and, when appropriate, used in conjunction with subjective data to provide information about the states of nature in the problem and to assist the decision maker in assessing the probabilities of those states.

In this chapter we will examine certain aspects of empirical data that could be useful to the decision maker. These aspects include types of data, sources of data, and methods for evaluating and obtaining certain useful information from the data. Most procedures for obtaining information from data are considered to be statistical. It is not the purpose of this book to present a course in statistics or even an overview of statistical methods. Any manager who desires to use precise statistical techniques for analyzing data can find detailed instruction in any textbook on applied statistics. This chapter provides only some rough, approximate methods which are consistent with the intuitive approach to decision making. Some of these methods might be classified as "eyeballing"—that is, making estimates simply by looking at the data. Others involve a little more arithmetic, but nothing that can't be done quickly and easily by any managerial decision maker.

THE NATURE OF DATA

We may occasionally hear the word "data" applied to written descriptions of situations, events, or other phenomena. In general, however, the term refers to numbers. These numbers result from observing various types of transactions or occurrences and recording the result of each observation numerically. This process of observation may be part of a planned survey or experiment or it may result from the performance of some other function unrelated to the decision maker's problem. An example of the latter is recordkeeping for accounting purposes. However, regardless of the purpose for which they were originally obtained, numerical data result logically from all types of activities performed by organizations.

Numbers represent prices and quantities of products produced and sold. They represent hours worked, hours absent, and accrued sick leave. Numbers stand for taxes collected or paid, dollars of sales and returns, and balances of delinquent accounts. Numbers also represent customers, inventories, costs and profits, assets and liabilities, and income and expenses. In short, information about every possible business transaction can be represented by numbers. Whenever numbers are collected and recorded, regardless of what they represent, they become data.

Managers frequently receive large quantities of data in the course of their day-to-day activities. These data contain information that may reflect the status of some operational unit, such as a retail store, a brokerage office, a department in a manufacturing firm, or a government bureau. They may also reflect the status of some critical operating factor within that unit, such as sales, debt, absenteeism, or costs of one kind or another. The information may be in the form of reports or computer printouts, or it may simply consist of records kept in ledgers or file folders. In whatever form the data exist, they contain information about the transactions from which they resulted. The ability of a manager to extract useful information from such data can have a significant effect on his decision making.

At this point it is important to distinguish between two concepts related to data: populations and samples. A set of data represents a *population* if it consists of all the possible observations or data elements of a particular kind that are of interest to the decision maker. For example, if the decision maker is interested in the income characteristics of all families living in New York City, the population is the set of incomes of every family residing in New York City. If the decision maker is interested in the prices of all stocks listed on the New York Stock Exchange as of closing on October 25, the population consists of the prices of that complete set of stocks. Under other circumstances, the decision maker may be interested in the market for a particular type of product. In that case, the population is the complete set of individuals who might purchase that product. In obtaining information pertinent to a decision situation, the decision maker is concerned with populations—or, more precisely, with the characteristics of populations.

Rarely does a decision maker have access to data that represent complete populations. It is more likely that the available data represent only part of a population. Such data are called a *sample*. Most planned studies, such as market surveys, utilize samples, since populations are usually too large for an observation to be made on every member. Characteristics of a population can be inferred from a sample provided that it is representative of the population from which it was obtained. The selection of representative samples is a complex statistical technique and will not be discussed here. It is important, however, that the decision maker consider the representativeness of the sample when drawing conclusions about population characteristics. If the sample is not representative of the population from which it came, it is said to be *biased*. Inferences made from biased samples can lead to erroneous conclusions.

Bias results when the sample is restricted to certain population elements and excludes others. For example, if the population of registered voters in a particular district is sampled by selecting names from a telephone directory, the sample will most likely be biased. Registered voters who do not have telephones would automatically be excluded and voters with more than one phone listed would have a much greater chance of being included. The classic example of biased sampling is the *Literary Digest* poll that attempted to predict the result of the 1936 presidential election. In that poll, questionnaires were sent to a sample of people whose names were selected from telephone directories and automobile registration lists. As a result of the poll, the *Literary Digest* predicted that the winner of the election would be Alfred Landon, the Republican candidate. In fact, Franklin Roosevelt, the Democrat, won by a landslide, taking every state except Maine and Vermont. By selecting the sample from telephone directories and automobile registration lists, particularly in a period of economic depression, the *Digest* excluded that large segment of the population that could afford neither telephones nor automobiles. Since votes in that election were cast largely along economic lines, the portion of the population that was excluded from the sample had a significant effect on the results of the election.

Suppose that information is required about the characteristics of the population of shoppers who patronize a particular suburban shopping mall. Data are obtained from interviews conducted with a sample of shoppers on a single Wednesday afternoon.

The result is likely to be biased, since people who work and must shop evenings or weekends are automatically excluded. Of course, if there is reason to believe that Wednesday afternoon shoppers are typical of all patrons of the mall, the bias might not be significant and the sample might be representative. In the final analysis, it is the decision maker who must judge the representativeness of the sample data. Sometimes, particularly when the data do not result from a planned study, biased data are used simply because no other data are available. Once again, the decision maker must judge how such biased data are to be used in order to avoid making poor decisions. Generally, when data are known to be biased but the nature of the bias is also known, conclusions can be modified to account for the bias. Also, when the data are biased or the sample cannot be assumed to be representative, the data should be used to supplement the decision maker's subjective information, not as the sole source of decision-making information.

The *currency* of data is another important aspect that must be considered. The decision maker should be aware that populations are not necessarily static. Characteristics of populations change over time. Population data obtained a year ago may not be representative of the population as it exists today. The same thing is true of data from an unbiased sample that is outdated.

Data can be classified according to type—that is, qualitative or quantitative. When observations are made of some characteristic of a single population element, the result is not always a number. Characteristics that cannot be represented by a numerical value are called *qualitative* characteristics, or *attributes*. An attribute cannot be measured or counted; only its presence or absence can be observed. Attributes of customers of a suburban shopping mall that would be of interest to a decision maker might include sex, race, and home ownership. Although each customer could be classified into one of two or more categories, there is no numerical value that is inherently associated with such a classification. What number would you associate with the category of female as opposed to male, or with the racial categories of white, black, and Oriental?

When dealing with qualitative or attributes data, numerical

values are obtained by counting the number of observations or units that fall in each of the mutually exclusive categories of the attribute. For example, we could report that out of 100 customers interviewed, 65 were homeowners and 35 were not. Or, out of the same 100, 45 were registered Democrats, 30 were registered Republicans, 15 were registered as independents, and 10 were not registered. The number aggregated in each category is often associated with a proportion or a percentage. That is, we could say that of the 100 customers interviewed, 65% were homeowners and 35% were not. Or, the percentage in the voting registration categories were 45%, 30%, 15%, and 10% respectively.

On the other hand, when a number can be naturally associated with a characteristic of one of the observed elements by a process of measuring or counting, that characteristic is said to be quantitative and is called a *variable*. The data resulting from observations of a variable are called variables data. Height, weight, price, income, number of members in the family, and hours worked per week are all quantitative characteristics or variables.

In the preceding chapter we indicated that the normal distribution can be used to help the decision maker assign probabilities to the states of nature in his decision situation provided that the states can be represented by numerical values. Using the present terminology, this means that the states of nature can be represented by values of a variable. If the states are categorical (that is, attributes), the normal distribution cannot be used and the decision maker must resort to the betting-odds method of assessing probabilities.

In general, then, data can represent total populations or partial populations (called samples). They may have been collected for the express purpose of assisting the decision-making process or they may be the result of some recordkeeping operation that is unrelated to the decision problem. Regardless of the reason the data were originally obtained, the information they contain can often be useful to the manager in the decision-making process. However, before the manager can use this information he must be able to extract it from the raw or unprocessed data. We will discuss some simple methods for doing this after we consider some of the data sources generally available.

SOURCES OF DATA

In keeping records of transactions, every business organization is constantly creating or generating data. These data become the raw material of decision making. In fact, unprocessed data that result from this process of observation are called *raw data.* The primary purpose of the methods we will discuss later in this chapter is to process raw data in order to make them more intelligible and to extract information that is useful in making decisions.

The most important source of data for making decisions is the organization's own records of its activities and business transactions. Sometimes, however, it is necessary to go outside the organization to collect information from customers, suppliers, or other parties. Any planned program for collecting data, whether within or outside the organization, is generally referred to as a survey. When observations are made on every member of the population of interest, the survey is called a census. If observations are made on a sample drawn from the population, the survey is referred to as a sample survey. Well-designed surveys represent the best source of information for decision makers. However, in most decision situations, there is usually neither the time nor funds available for conducting surveys, and the decision maker must rely on whatever information is readily available.

Large quantities of useful data for decision making can often be obtained from various organizations. The federal government is probably the most prolific generator of statistical data and reports. Trade associations are a somewhat distant second. None of these sources should be overlooked in the search for information.

Published statistical reports are frequently divided into primary and secondary sources. A primary source is the agency that actually collects the data and first publishes them. A secondary source refers to a republication by some other organization or agency.

OTHER IMPORTANT ASPECTS OF DATA

The primary objective of the decision maker in dealing with large sets of data is to organize and summarize the data in a way that allows him to obtain useful information. There are many things that can be done to summarize, describe, and extract information from large data sets. We will discuss only the simplest and quickest of the approximating methods which are most useful to the intuitive decision maker.

Whenever observations are made of a population element and recorded numerically, information is obtained about that particular element as well as about the population to which that element belongs. Each observation contains a bit of information. An entire population of observations contains all the information available in the population about the particular characteristic that was observed. There is no way to extract more information from a set of data than was in the data to begin with. In order to create something from nothing, one would have to be a magician. However, procedures do exist to obtain information from data sets in a usable form and in the most efficient and economical way. Some of these procedures concentrate on describing the entire data set; others concentrate on measuring a single facet or characteristic of the set. The characteristics of data sets that we will be concerned with are shape, variability, and location.

The shape of a particular data distribution can be compared with the shape of the normal distribution, discussed in the previous chapter. If there is a reasonable amount of similarity between the two, we can use what is known about the characteristics of the normal distribution to draw conclusions about the data set at hand and about the population it represents. The shape is most conveniently discerned from frequency tables and frequency graphs, which will be discussed shortly.

The degree to which members of a' population differ from one another is probably the most important characteristic of a population. Such differences appear to be inherent in nature. No two objects are ever exactly alike. Even in a manufacturing process, variation occurs among parts or products turned out from a single set of plans and specifications. Every unit produced is always slightly different from every other one. Consequently, in describing a set of data, some measure of variation is required.

Location refers to the position of the data on a scale of numerical values. For example, wages earned by production workers in a large manufacturing company may range from $3.50 per hour for unskilled workers to $9.75 per hour for highly skilled technicians. The scale of numbers which describes these wages must run from 3.50 to 9.75. A lathe operator's wages may be located on this scale between the values 5.75 and 6.25.

A useful measure for summarizing the general location of the set of numbers is a central value, such as a mean or a median. In a sense, such a value is representative of the entire set. If a decision maker had to select a single number that was most representative of the set, it would probably be the mean or the median.

Once measures of location and variation have been determined for a set of data and the distribution has been displayed in tabular or graphic form, the decision maker can obtain a reasonably good description of the data set. In the following sections we will discuss some simple methods for obtaining these descriptions.

FREQUENCY TABLES AND GRAPHS

Raw data consist of a large number of observations recorded in the form of numbers. Before the data are manipulated or processed in some way, they appear in no particular order or arrangement that would enable anyone to obtain useful information from them. Nevertheless, these data do contain information that can and should be useful in the decision-making process. Every manager should be aware of some of the techniques for extracting information from large sets of data even though he may not be required to do the processing himself. Even more important, every manager should know the kinds of information that are useful in decision making and should be able to use some quick, approximate methods for obtaining that information when there just isn't enough time for more complete formal processing.

Suppose, for example, that data have been collected on the number of hours of overtime worked during one month by 5,000 production employees of a large manufacturing company. The data have been requested by the production vice president to provide information bearing on many kinds of decisions he must make involving production schedules, new business, hiring of personnel, plant expansions, and equipment purchases. The data have been printed out by a computer which simply scanned each employee record in its memory and printed the number of overtime hours worked during the specified month. However, having simply requested a list of these hours, with no additional information, the vice president is now confronted with 5,000 numbers listed by employee name and Social Security number. These data contain useful information. However, the arrangement of the numbers is completely unrelated to their magnitude or to any other characteristic of the data which would provide the manager with useful information from the data set whether he does it himself or instructs the computer to do it for him.

A set of data need not contain 5,000 numbers in order to be incomprehensible. Even as few as 50 numbers can be confusing. Suppose that the president of Eastways, the manufacturer's representative discussed previously, has asked for some marketing information about the new product that the company is considering adding to its present line. Although the product in question is relatively new on the market, 50 other representatives in various parts of the country have already been marketing it for a year, and the manufacturer is willing to supply these sales figures to Eastways. The data reporting the first-year sales in units for the 50 representatives are shown in Table 8.1. These data are rounded to the nearest 10 units.

Before any useful information can be obtained from the data, it is necessary to rearrange them, listing the numbers in order of magnitude—that is, from largest to smallest or from smallest to largest. When the data are arranged in that manner, the table is called an *array,* as illustrated in Table 8.2.

When raw data are arranged in an array, some of their characteristics immediately become evident. For example, the range of the data is very easy to obtain. The number of units sold by the 50 manufacturer's representatives during 1980 varies

TABLE 8.1   Sales in units,
1/1/80 through 12/31/80—raw data.

3,000	5,500	4,750	3,900	2,500
3,200	3,800	4,800	5,400	2,250
4,200	5,400	2,100	4,600	5,300
6,000	4,150	5,000	4,400	2,200
3,250	3,650	4,300	4,750	3,900
5,750	3,200	5,250	4,300	2,650
4,300	3,350	2,500	5,400	4,900
4,400	5,250	3,700	3,100	4,100
2,900	4,000	3,000	3,000	4,400
4,600	3,600	4,800	4,500	4,750

from a low of 2,100 to a high of 6,000. The range is the difference between these two extreme values, or 3,900.

The array also makes it easy to locate the midpoint, or middle value, of the set. To find the middle value, which is called the *median*, start at either end of the array and locate a point that divides the data set into two equal parts—that is, half the values fall above that point and half fall below it. Since there are 50 numbers in Table 8.2, a point that divides the set in half must fall between the two middle numbers, that is, between the 25th and 26th numbers from either end. The two middle numbers in this array are 4,200 and 4,300. By convention, the median is said to be the value of the point halfway between the two middle numbers—in this case, 4,250. If there happened to be an odd number of values in the data set, the median would coincide with the middle value. The median is an average and can be considered to be a representative value. In other words, 4,250

TABLE 8.2   Sales in units, 1/1/80 through
12/31/80—arranged in order of magnitude.

2,100	3,100	3,900	4,400	5,000
2,200	3,200	4,000	4,500	5,250
2,250	3,200	4,100	4,600	5,250
2,500	3,250	4,150	4,600	5,300
2,500	3,350	4,200	4,750	5,400
2,650	3,600	4,300	4,750	5,400
2,900	3,650	4,300	4,750	5,400
3,000	3,700	4,300	4,800	5,500
3,000	3,800	4,400	4,800	5,750
3,000	3,900	4,400	4,900	6,000

units is fairly representative of the first-year sales figures of these 50 representatives.

Although it is easy to find the median and the range from the array, it is impossible to discern anything about the shape of the distribution of the data. Therefore, it is desirable to construct a *frequency table* or *frequency distribution* and then to draw a graph of the distribution. A frequency distribution is constructed by dividing the range of values covered by the data into segments or classes, preferably of equal length, and then recording the number of observations that fall into each class. The number of observations in each class is called the frequency.

Determining the number of classes to have in a frequency distribution is somewhat arbitrary and depends largely on the judgment of the individual analyzing the data. There are, however, certain guidelines that should be followed:

1. A frequency distribution should consist of at least 5 and not more than 20 classes. Too few classes or too many classes will tend to obscure the characteristics of the data rather than highlight them—which is, after all, the purpose of the frequency distribution.

2. Since each class covers a finite range of values, called the class interval, the number of classes and the interval should be chosen so that the observations are distributed fairly evenly throughout each class. If any clustering of observations does occur, it should occur near the middle of the intervals.

3. The classes chosen must be all-inclusive—that is, they must cover the entire range of values in the data set. The classes may, in fact, cover a slightly greater range than the actual values. The lowest class may begin slightly below the smallest value in the set and the highest class may extend slightly above the largest value in the set.

4. The classes must be mutually exclusive. Every observation must fall into one and only one class.

5. The number of classes and the class interval should be chosen to avoid the occurrence of empty classes—that is, classes with 0 frequencies.

6. It is desirable to have class intervals that are the same size for all classes.

In Table 8.3, the sales data have been grouped into two

TABLE 8.3 Frequency distributions of units sold, 1/1/80 through 12/31/80.

Frequency Distribution *a*			Frequency Distribution *b*		
Class	Freq.	Class Midpoint	Class	Freq.	Class Midpoint
2,000–2,590	5	2,295	2,000–2,690	6	2,345
2,600–3,190	6	2,895	2,700–3,390	9	3,045
3,200–3,790	7	3,495	3,400–4,090	7	3,745
3,800–4,390	10	4,095	4,100–4,790	15	4,445
4,400–4,990	12	4,695	4,800–5,490	10	5,145
5,000–5,590	8	5,295	5,500–6,190	3	5,845
5,600–6,190	2	5,895		50	
	50				

different frequency distributions to illustrate the point that there is no single, correct frequency distribution for a given set of data. As long as a frequency distribution follows the guidelines listed above and provides a clear description of the data distribution, it is correct. Notice that frequency distribution *a* has seven classes while frequency distribution *b* has only six. Each class in the first distribution covers an interval of 600 units, while each class in the second distribution covers an interval of 700 units. The largest and the smallest values that belong to any class are called the class limits, and the class interval is obtained by finding the difference between any two adjacent upper or lower class limits. Notice that the range of values covered by these two frequency distributions is slightly greater than that of the raw data. The lower class limit of the lowest class in the frequency distributions is 2,000 while the smallest value in the data set is 2,100. Also, the upper class limit of the highest class is 6,190 while the largest value in the data set is 6,000. For simplicity's sake we have assumed that the data have been rounded to the nearest 10 units. That is, a number such as 3,995 was rounded and recorded as 4,000; a number such as 3,254 was rounded and recorded as 3,250.

The construction of a frequency distribution can be simplified by using a tally sheet, as illustrated in Figure 8.1 for the frequency distributions of Table 8.3. This is simply a recording form in which a row is assigned to each class in the frequency distribution and is identified by a value corresponding to the

FIGURE 8.1 Tally sheets for recording frequencies.

Frequency Tally Sheet									
Data: Sales in units									
Source: Atlas Mfg. Co.							Date: 2/1/81		
Class	Value	Frequencies							
1	2,295	XX	XX	X					
2	2,895	XX	XX	XX					
3	3,495	XX	XX	XX	X				
4	4,095	XX	XX	XX	XX	XX			
5	4,695	XX	XX	XX	XX	XX	XX		
6	5,295	XX	XX	XX	XX				
7	5,895	XX							

Frequency Distribution *a*

Frequency Tally Sheet									
Data: Sales in units									
Source: Atlas Mfg. Co.							Date: 2/1/81		
Class	Value	Frequencies							
1	2,345	XX	XX	XX					
2	3,045	XX	XX	XX	XX	X			
3	3,745	XX	XX	XX	X				
4	4,445	XX	XX	XX	XX	XX	XX	XX	X
5	5,145	XX	XX	XX	XX	XX			
6	5,845	XX	X						

Frequency Distribution *b*

midpoint of the class; the columns are provided to facilitate recording the frequencies. When each measurement or observation is obtained, a mark is made in the appropriate row. These marks can be check marks, 1's, X's or any other convenient symbol. X's have been used in the illustration. When all the data have been entered on the tally sheet, a count of the frequencies is made. An added advantage of the tally sheet is that it provides a rough picture of the distribution pattern.

Even though the pattern of the distribution is apparent from the tally sheet, in order to compare that pattern with a normal distribution, we will need another type of display. This is the *histogram*. A histogram is a graph in which the horizontal axis represents the values of the observations and the vertical scale represents the frequencies. Each class in the frequency distribution is represented by a vertical rectangle or bar whose base corresponds to the class interval and whose height is proportional to the frequency in that class. Histograms picturing the frequency distributions of Table 8.3 are shown in Figure 8.2. Notice that there are no spaces between the bars.

THE PRACTICAL USE
OF FREQUENCY TABLES AND GRAPHS

The primary purpose of constructing frequency distributions and histograms is to summarize large quantities of raw numerical data. For the decision maker who uses data to obtain information about the states of nature in his decision situation and to assess the probabilities associated with those states, frequency distributions help the decision maker determine if the population from which the data were obtained has a normal or approximately normal distribution. This is the same normal distribution that was discussed in Chapter 7. For populations that have normal distributions, the probabilities associated with values or intervals of values can easily be determined by converting the values to Z scores and obtaining the probabilities from the table of the standard normal distribution. Of course, the normal distribution is a theoretical concept, and most populations are not precisely normal. However, many empirical distributions are approx-

FIGURE 8.2 Histograms of distributions of units sold.

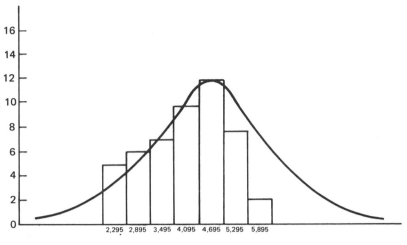

Frequency Distribution *a*

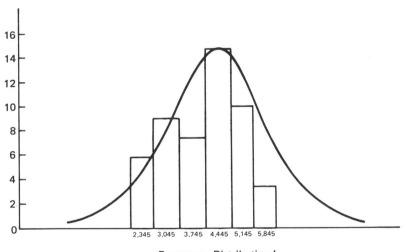

Frequency Distribution *b*

imately normal in the sense that the greatest concentration of values occurs near the mean or middle value and the frequencies decrease the further one departs from that middle value in either direction.

Data available to the decision maker are usually a sample that has been drawn from the population of interest. However, if it is a representative sample, its distribution can be used to judge whether the population it represents is, at least, approximately normal. As an example, normal curves have been superimposed on the histograms of the sales data available to Eastways and shown in Figure 8.2. Although it is apparent that the normal curve is not an exact fit to these data, we might be inclined to assume that it is a reasonable approximation and could be used to help in assessing probabilities.

If the graph or histogram appears to deviate too greatly from the normal distribution for the decision maker to be comfortable with the assumption of normality, then probability assessments can be based on the relative frequency in each class. The relative frequency is simply the proportion of the total number of observations that fall in the class and is obtained by dividing each class frequency by the total number of observations in the data set. Table 8.4 shows the frequency distributions of Table 8.3 with the relative frequencies added.

Remember, particularly when the data represent a sample, that any value obtained from the data is at best an approxima-

TABLE 8.4   Frequency distributions of units sold, with relative frequencies.

Frequency Distribution *a*			Frequency Distribution *b*		
Class	Freq.	Relative Frequency	Class	Freq.	Relative Frequency
2,000–2,590	5	5/50 = .10	2,000–2,690	6	6/50 = .12
2,600–3,190	6	6/50 = .12	2,700–3,390	9	9/50 = .18
3,200–3,790	7	7/50 = .14	3,400–4,090	7	7/50 = .14
3,800–4,390	10	10/50 = .20	4,100–4,790	15	15/50 = .30
4,400–4,990	12	12/50 = .24	4,800–5,490	10	10/50 = .20
5,000–5,590	8	8/50 = .16	5,500–6,190	3	3/50 = .06
5,600–6,190	2	2/50 = .04		50	1.00
	50	1.00			

tion. In the formal intuitive method of decision making, probability estimates are based on the decision maker's judgment rather than on precise statistical methods. In other words, the data are an adjunct to, not a substitute for, the decision maker's judgment.

Figure 8.3 shows several different frequency patterns. It would appear that patterns 1 through 5 could reasonably be approximated with a normal distribution. Patterns 6 and 7 appear doubtful, and patterns 8 and 9 are not likely candidates.

DESCRIPTIVE MEASURES
OF LOCATION AND VARIATION

A measure of location and variation in conjunction with a frequency table or graph can provide the decision maker with a reasonably accurate picture of a data set. If the frequency patterns suggest that the distribution is at least approximately normal, probabilities can be determined—provided that the mean and standard deviation of the population from which the data were obtained are known or can be estimated.

The mean, or arithmetic mean, is the value that most people think of when the term "average" is used. There are, in fact, several different types of averages, of which the arithmetic mean is only one. This mean is computed by adding all the values in the set of data and dividing the sum by the number of elements in the set. For example, if we designate the characteristic being observed with the letter X, the arithmetic mean of all the X's is designated $\bar{X}$ (pronounced X bar) and is defined by:

$$\bar{X} = \frac{\Sigma X}{n}$$

where Σ is a symbol meaning "sum" and n represents the number of elements in the set.

Although $\bar{X}$ is the best estimate of the population mean, another type of average, the median, can also be used and is much simpler to obtain. In fact, when the data are normally distributed, the mean and the median have identical values. When a set has an odd number of elements, the median, desig-

FIGURE 8.3 Frequency patterns.

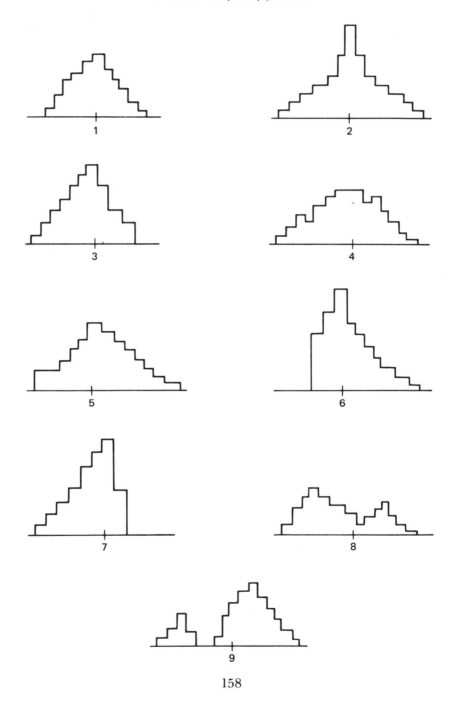

nated M, is the middle value of the set. When a set has an even number of elements, the median is halfway between the two middle values. Once the data have been arranged into an array, the middle values can be determined by counting.

For the set of 50 sales figures in the array of Table 8.2, the two middle values are 4,200 and 4,300 and the value that lies halfway between is 4,250. This is the median. If we were to compute the arithmetic mean from the same set of data, we would get $\bar{X} = 4,100$. Although the mean can be computed fairly easily from small data sets and can be obtained from a computer when the set is large, the convenience of being able to obtain the median at practically a glance outweighs its disadvantages when used in the formal intuitive decision-making procedure. Also, arguments can be made to favor the median over the mean as a measure of location for the data set and as a representative value.

The most common measure of variation of a set of data is the standard deviation. Again, because of the amount of computation involved in obtaining this value, we will provide simple methods for estimating the standard deviation based on ranges or modified ranges. Remember that the range is simply the difference between the largest and smallest values in a set. That is:

$$R = X_L - X_S$$

We have already determined that the range of the data from Table 8.2 is $R = 6,000 - 2,100 = 3,900$.

When the data consist of 100 or fewer observations, the *average range method* is used to estimate the standard deviation. In this method, the *original* set of data is randomly divided into subgroups of equal size. The range is determined for each of the subgroups and the average range, $\bar{R}$, is obtained by adding up the subgroup ranges and dividing by the number of subgroups. That is:

$$\bar{R} = \frac{\Sigma R}{k}$$

where k represents the number of subgroups.

An estimate of the standard deviation is given by:

$$S = \frac{\bar{R}}{f}$$

where f is a factor that can be obtained from Table 8.5 for subgroup sizes from $n = 2$ to $n = 100$.

Refer again to the original sales data in Table 8.1. It would be convenient to divide these data into five subgroups of ten elements each. Since the raw data are in no particular order and have not been processed in any way, we can simply let each subgroup correspond to one column. Then the ranges of the five subgroups are as follows:

$$
\begin{aligned}
R_1 &= 6,000 - 2,900 = 3,100 \\
R_2 &= 5,500 - 3,200 = 2,300 \\
R_3 &= 5,250 - 2,100 = 3,150 \\
R_4 &= 5,400 - 3,000 = 2,400 \\
R_5 &= 5,300 - 2,200 = \underline{3,100} \\
& 14,050
\end{aligned}
$$

The average range is $\bar{R} = 14,050/5 = 2,810$.

The factor f for subgroups of size 10 is 3.078 (from Table 8.5). Therefore, the estimated standard deviation is $S = 2,810/3.078 = 912.93$, or 913. The true standard deviation of this set of data is actually about 930.

When the set of data consists of 100 or more observations, there is another method for estimating the standard deviation that does not require the use of a table. This is referred to as the 7% *method.* Using an array of the data, find the two values that divide the lowest 7% of the observations and the highest 7% of the observations from all the others. For example, if there are 100 observations in the set and this method is used, 7% of 100 is 7. Therefore, we would find the eighth value from both ends, since 7 values will fall below the eighth lowest value and 7 values will fall above the eighth highest value. We then find the difference between those two values and divide that difference by 3. The result is an estimate of the standard deviation.

Rather than illustrate this procedure with an entirely new set of data, we will use the 50 values in the array of Table 8.2. In practice, however, this method should not be used unless there are at least 100 elements in the set. Since 7% of 50 is 3.5 and

TABLE 8.5   Factors for estimating the standard deviation
from the average range.

Number of Observations in Subgroup n	Estimating Factor f	Number of Observations in Subgroup n	Estimating Factor f
2	1.128	21	3.778
3	1.693	22	3.819
4	2.059	23	3.858
5	2.326	24	3.895
6	2.534	25	3.931
7	2.704	30	4.086
8	2.857	35	4.213
9	2.970	40	4.322
10	3.078	45	4.415
11	3.173	50	4.498
12	3.258	55	4.572
13	3.336	60	4.639
14	3.407	65	4.699
15	3.472	70	4.755
16	3.532	75	4.806
17	3.588	80	4.854
18	3.640	85	4.898
19	3.689	90	4.939
20	3.735	95	4.978
		100	5.015

there is no such thing as half of an observation, we select the fourth lowest and fourth highest values in the array. The fourth lowest value is 2,500 and the fourth highest is 5,400. The difference between these two values, which we call a modified range, or R', is $R' = 5,400 - 2,500 = 2,900$.

The estimated standard deviation is obtained by dividing this modified range by 3, and for these data that value is $S = R'/3 = 2,900/3 = 966.7$, or approximately 967. The estimated value would be closer to the true value if there were more than 100 observations in the data set rather than only 50. Also, the estimate is better for normal or near normal distributions than for distributions that differ significantly from normal.

ACCURACY AND JUDGMENT

The methods we have discussed for summarizing and describing large sets of empirical data are not exact or precise. However, they were not intended to be. Precision has been sacrificed in the interest of convenience and simplicity. Whenever a decision maker believes that precise statistical methods are called for, he should consult a good textbook on applied statistics. These approximate methods should be used as an adjunct to the decision maker's judgment. The empirical data represent a source of information for the decision maker, but not the sole source. The other important source of information is subjective data.

In the formal intuitive method, major emphasis is placed on the judgment of the decision maker. Therefore, it is most important that the final probability distribution on the states of nature in the decision situation be consistent with the decision maker's true feelings about these probabilities. Remember that in subscribing to the subjective view of probability, we reject the idea that there is a single, objective probability distribution that is correct and that all others are incorrect. Any empirical data that bear on the situation have value primarily in either reinforcing or modifying the subjective information that the decision maker brings to the problem. The summarizing and descriptive measures we have discussed are simply tools to help the decision maker comprehend the important characteristics of those empirical data.

As previously mentioned, the consequences in most decision situations are relatively insensitive to small changes in the probabilities assigned to the individual states. Most decision makers cannot really interpret small differences in probability values, such as the difference between .71 and .73. Consequently, the value of these techniques lies not in their ability to produce very precise probabilities but rather in their consistency and the systematic and logical reasoning that they require of the decision maker. Criticism can be leveled at the rough estimating procedures described in this chapter, but experience indicates that in most decision situations the manager has neither the time nor the inclination to apply precise statistical methods.

This should not be construed as an argument against using precise methods. However, if such methods are to be used in any decision analysis, they should be used throughout. That is, they should be used in the design of the experiment or sampling plan for obtaining data; in the collection of the data; and in the analysis of the data. If such precise methods are used, the decision maker should probably consult with a statistician, since the incorrect use of statistical techniques can lead to incorrect and undesirable results.

The Eastways Case

In the preceding chapter, the president of Eastways subjectively determined that sales of the new product line could be approximated with a normal distribution and arrived at estimates of 4,500 units for the mean and 1,100 units for the standard deviation. Probabilities for each level of sales (that is, each state of nature) were obtained from the table of the standard normal distribution. The empirical data on sales provided in this chapter are not inconsistent with those subjective estimates. The histograms of the frequency patterns of sales in Figure 8.2 are certainly not precisely normal, but considering the relatively small number of observations, they appear to be close enough to pattern 3 in Figure 8.3 to justify use of the normal distribution.

The median of 4,250 obtained from these data is reasonably close to the decision maker's judgmental mean of 4,500, and the estimated standard deviation of 913 is not too much different from the subjective estimate of 1,100. If after observing the data, the president of Eastways still feels comfortable about the distribution obtained in Chapter 7, he would be wise to let it stand.

If, on the other hand, he is uneasy about the differences between his subjective estimates and those obtained from the data, particularly the difference in the two estimates of the standard deviation, he might want to reassess and possibly modify his subjective distribution. However, since there is reasonable agreement between the two sets of estimates, it is unlikely that a reassessment would result in substantial modifications to his subjective distribution. It is also unlikely that minor changes in the state probabilities would affect the final decision.

9

THE FORMAL INTUITIVE METHOD

The formal intuitive method of decision making is a logical and consistent procedure for selecting an optimal course of action from a set of available alternatives. It is also a fairly simple procedure. Any complexities that a decision maker may encounter in applying this technique result from the complexities inherent in the decision situation, not from the formal intuitive method itself. The components of this method are (1) the description of the situation with a payoff table or decision tree, (2) the selection of a decision criterion, (3) the assessment and allocation of probabilities to the states of nature, and (4) the application of the decision criterion to the selection of an optimal act.

In Chapter 5 various decision criteria were examined. Discussion of the most important one, the expected value criterion, was postponed because the topic of probability had not yet been covered. Before the expected value criterion can be used, probabilities must be assigned to each state of nature. In this chapter we will describe the expected value criterion and complete the formal intuitive method.

164

THE EXPECTED VALUE CRITERION— THE WEIGHTED AVERAGE

The selection of an optimal act from a set of alternatives is facilitated if the acts can be compared against a single value that is in some way representative of the consequences of the act. For the three criteria of optimism, pessimism, and neutrality, discussed in Chapter 5, the representative value of each act was dependent on the decision maker's assessment of the state probabilities even though his choice of probability values was extremely limited under those criteria. Now, however, we have learned how to assign a wide range of probability values to the states of nature in the form of a probability distribution. With this new ability, we can determine a much more reasonable representative value for each act. This value will be called the *expected value* of the act, and it is simply the weighted average of the conditional consequences of the act where the weights are the probabilities assigned to the states.

The term "expected value" should be intuitively appealing to the decision maker, since it connotes an expected or likely result under the conditions of uncertainty inherent in the decision situation. When applied to decision situations that recur with some frequency, the expected value represents a long-term average consequence. For one-of-a-kind situations, a long-term average is not a practical interpretation. In these unique and nonprogrammable decision situations, the decision maker should interpret the expected value as a most likely result that can be used as a representative value of an act and that facilitates comparisons among the available acts.

We will represent the expected value of an act with the notation EV followed by parentheses enclosing the symbol for the act. For example, $EV(a_1)$ represents the expected value of the act a_1. In some instances a brief description of the act will be used rather than a symbol. For example, if in a particular decision situation a choice must be made between the acts "accept the offer" and "reject the offer," the expected values of these acts may be designated EV(accept) and EV(reject).

The expected value of an act is obtained by multiplying each conditional consequence of the act for a given state by the probability assigned to that state and then adding the results. Very simply, if there are two acts, a_1 and a_2, and five states of nature, s_1 through s_5, and if the conditional consequences and probabilities are as shown in Figure 9.1, then the expected value of each act is obtained as follows:

$$EV(a_1) = (.25)(-1,000) + (.30)(2,000) + (.20)(3,000)$$
$$+ (.15)(4,000) + (.10)(5,000)$$
$$= -250 + 600 + 600 + 600 + 500$$
$$= 2,050$$

$$EV(a_2) = (.25)(3,000) + (.30)(1,000) + (.20)(2,000)$$
$$+ (.15)(4,000) + (.10)(-500)$$
$$= 750 + 300 + 400 + 600 - 50$$
$$= 2,000$$

The expected value criterion specifies that the act with the highest expected value is the optimal alternative in the decision situation. Thus, for the data summarized in the payoff table of Figure 9.1, a_1 is the better of the two acts, since $EV(a_1) = 2,050$ is greater than $EV(a_2) = 2,000$. Notice that there are negative values among the conditional consequences of both acts. These negative payoffs represent losses or costs as contrasted with profits or gains.

THE EXPECTED VALUE CRITERION IN SINGLE-STAGE DECISION SITUATIONS

We will now demonstrate how the expected value criterion is applied to the single-stage decision situations described in Chapter 4. Remember that a single-stage decision situation is one in which the problem is resolved by a single decision made at a specific point in time. Single-stage decision situations are best described with payoff tables.

All the cases we will discuss have been analyzed step by step in earlier chapters as we proceeded through the various stages of the formal intuitive method. Each decision situation was described with an appropriate table or diagram and probabilities

FIGURE 9.1   Payoff table with probabilities.

STATES	PROBABILITIES	ACTS	
		a_1	a_2
s_1	$P(s_1) =$ .25	$-1,000$	3,000
s_2	$P(s_2) =$ .30	2,000	1,000
s_3	$P(s_3) =$ .20	3,000	2,000
s_4	$P(s_4) =$ .15	4,000	4,000
s_5	$P(s_5) =$ .10	5,000	-500
	1.00	EV 2,050	2,000

were assigned to the states of nature. The assessment of probabilities was not shown for all the cases but was illustrated in Chapter 7 for the Eastways case.

The final stage of the procedure is to use the expected value criterion to select the optimal act. We will begin each of the following examples by reproducing the appropriate payoff tables with the state probabilities added. It is recommended that the reader review each of the cases before proceeding.

The EDI Case

Executives of Electronic Devices, Inc. must make a decision in response to a request for a proposal from a government agency. Initially, they defined the decision situation as a two-action, two-state situation in which their alternatives were simply "bid" and "decline to bid." The states of nature related to their success or failure in obtaining the contract. However, after several discussions between the decision maker and an assistant, the original decision situation was revised to include the possibility of bidding at one of three price levels in addition to not bidding at all. The states were also expanded to include success or failure in obtaining the contract at each price level. A summary of the final decision situation shows that the alternatives are:

a_1: high bid
a_2: moderate bid
a_3: low bid
a_4: no bid

The states in the problem are:

s_1:   EDI gets contract with high, moderate, or low bid
s_2:   EDI gets contract with moderate or low bid
s_3:   EDI gets contract with low bid
s_4:   EDI doesn't get contract

Using the betting-odds method of assessing probabilities, the decision maker arrived at this probability distribution on the states of nature:

$$P(s_1) = .05$$
$$P(s_2) = .15$$
$$P(s_3) = .35$$
$$P(s_4) = .45$$

The decision situation is summarized in Figure 9.2. Notice that this is the same as the payoff table in Figure 4.4 with the probabilities added and the expected value of each act noted.

The expected value of each act is computed as follows:

$$
\begin{aligned}
EV(a_1) &= (.05)(\$475{,}000) + (.15)(-\$95{,}000) + (.35)(-\$95{,}000) \\
&\quad + (.45)(-\$95{,}000) \\
&= \$23{,}750 - \$14{,}250 - \$33{,}250 - \$42{,}750 \\
&= -\$66{,}500
\end{aligned}
$$

$$
\begin{aligned}
EV(a_2) &= (.05)(\$350{,}000) + (.15)(\$350{,}000) + (.35)(-\$95{,}000) \\
&\quad + (.45)(-\$95{,}000) \\
&= \$17{,}500 + \$52{,}500 - \$33{,}250 - \$42{,}750 \\
&= -\$6{,}000
\end{aligned}
$$

$$
\begin{aligned}
EV(a_3) &= (.05)(\$125{,}000) + (.15)(\$125{,}000) + (.35)(\$125{,}000) \\
&\quad + (.45)(-\$95{,}000) \\
&= \$26{,}000
\end{aligned}
$$

$$
\begin{aligned}
EV(a_4) &= (.05)(0) + (.15)(0) + (.35)(0) + (.45)(0) \\
&= 0
\end{aligned}
$$

Using the expected value of each act as a representative value, we can see that a_3, with an expected value of $26,000, is the best of the four alternatives. Consequently, EDI should submit a bid at the low price. Of course, the optimality of that act is dependent on the probability distribution assigned to the states. However, as long as that distribution reflects the true feelings

FIGURE 9.2   Payoff table for EDI bid decision.

STATES	PROBABILITIES	ACTS			
		a_1	a_2	a_3	a_4
s_1	.05	$475,000	$350,000	$125,000	$0
s_2	.15	−$ 95,000	$350,000	$125,000	$0
s_3	.35	−$ 95,000	−$ 95,000	$125,000	$0
s_4	.45	−$ 95,000	−$ 95,000	−$ 95,000	$0
	1.00	EV −$ 66,500	−$ 6,000	$ 26,000	$0

of the decision maker about the likelihood of occurrence of each state, he should act in accordance with the expected value criterion.

The Granger Case

Paul Granger has to decide whether to accept an offer of $600,-000 for his land from the Southeastern Mutual Life Insurance Company. The consequences of his decision will be affected by a decision of the state highway department on a proposed expressway route across Granger's property. This situation is a two-action, two-state problem in which Granger's alternatives are:

a_1: accept offer (of insurance company)
a_2: reject offer

The states are:

s_1: expressway route approved
s_2: expressway route not approved

The decision situation is summarized in the payoff table in Figure 9.3. This is the same as the table in Figure 4.5 with the probabilities and the expected values of the acts added.

Granger used the betting-odds method to assess the probabilities of the states in this situation and arrived at the following values:

$$P(s_1) = .35$$
$$P(s_2) = .65$$

FIGURE 9.3   Payoff table for Granger land decision.

STATES	PROBABILITIES	ACTS	
		a_1	a_2
s_1	.35	$600,000	$750,000
s_2	.65	$600,000	$475,000
	1.00	EV $600,000	$571,250

The expected values of the acts are computed as follows:

$$EV(a_1) = (.35)(\$600,000) + (.65)(\$600,000)$$
$$= \$210,000 + \$390,000$$
$$= \$600,000$$

$$EV(a_2) = (.35)(\$750,000) + (.65)(\$475,000)$$
$$= \$262,500 + \$308,750$$
$$= \$571,250$$

Since the expected value of a_1 is greater than that of a_2, Granger should accept the offer of Southeastern Mutual. In this case, the expected value of $600,000 certain is greater than $750,000 with a probability of .35 or $475,000 with a probability of .65.

The Thompson Case

Frank Thompson, proprietor of Frank Thompson & Associates, General Contractors, must decide whether to purchase up to five building lots in a new housing development. His alternatives in this situation are:

a_0: purchase no lots
a_1: purchase one lot
a_2: purchase two lots
a_3: purchase three lots
a_4: purchase four lots
a_5: purchase five lots

The states in this situation represent the demand for houses on the lots during the year following construction. That is:

s_0: demand for no houses
s_1: demand for one house
s_2: demand for two houses
s_3: demand for three houses
s_4: demand for four houses
s_5: demand for five houses

Thompson assessed the probabilities of these states with the betting-odds method. The procedure he used to arrive at his final probability distribution was illustrated in Chapter 7. The probabilities are:

$$P(s_0) = 0$$
$$P(s_1) = .05$$
$$P(s_2) = .30$$
$$P(s_3) = .40$$
$$P(s_4) = .20$$
$$P(s_5) = .05$$
$$\overline{1.00}$$

Since the states in this situation consist of six numerical values, Thompson might have considered using the normal probability distribution to determine the probabilities. However, after using the betting-odds method, Thompson was satisfied that this distribution reflected his personal feelings quite accurately and decided not to use the other method. Thompson's decision situation is summarized in Figure 9.4. This is the same as Figure 4.6 with the state probabilities and the expected values of the acts added.

FIGURE 9.4   Payoff table for Thompson decision situation.

STATES	PROBABILITIES	ACTS		
		a_0	a_1	a_2
s_0	0	$0	−$78,000	−$156,000
s_1	.05	$0	$17,000	−$ 61,000
s_2	.30	$0	$17,000	$ 34,000
s_3	.40	$0	$17,000	$ 34,000
s_4	.20	$0	$17,000	$ 34,000
s_5	.05	$0	$17,000	$ 34,000
	1.00	EV $0	$17,000	$ 29,250
		a_3	a_4	a_5
s_0	0	−$234,000	−$312,000	−$390,000
s_1	.05	−$139,000	−$217,000	−$295,000
s_2	.30	−$ 44,000	−$122,000	−$200,000
s_3	.40	$ 51,000	−$ 27,000	−$105,000
s_4	.20	$ 51,000	$ 68,000	−$ 10,000
s_5	.05	$ 51,000	$ 68,000	$ 85,000
	1.00	$ 13,000	−$ 41,250	−$114,500

The expected values of the acts are computed as follows:

$EV(a_0)$ = (0)(0) + (.05)(0) + (.30)(0) + (.40)(0)
        + (.20)(0) + (.05)(0)
      = 0

$EV(a_1)$ = (0)(−$78,000) + (.05)($17,000) + (.30)($17,000)
        + (.40)($17,000) + (.20)($17,000) + (.05)($17,000)
      = $17,000

$EV(a_2)$ = (0)(−$156,000) + (.05)(−$61,000) + (.30)($34,000)
        + (.40)($34,000) + (.20)($34,000) + (.05)($34,000)
      = $29,250

$EV(a_3)$ = (0)(−$234,000) + (.05)(−$139,000) + (.30)(−$44,000)
        + (40)($51,000) + (.20)($51,000) + (.05)($51,000)
      = $13,000

$EV(a_4)$ = (0)(−$312,000) + (.05)(−$217,000) + (.30)(−$122,000)
        + (.40)(−$27,000) + (.20)($68,000) + (.05)($68,000)
      = −$41,250

$EV(a_5)$ = (0)(−$390,000) + (.05)(−$295,000) + (.30)(−$200,000)
        + (.40)(−$105,000) + (.20)(−$10,000) + (.05)($85,000)
      = −$114,500

The optimal act is a_2, with an expected value of $29,250. Consequently, Thompson should purchase two of the lots offered and build two houses.

The Eastways Case

Eastways, a manufacturer's representative, must make a decision on a new product line it has been offered. In the analysis described in Chapter 4, the alternatives open to Eastways were:

a_1: accept the new product line and establish a separate division
a_2: accept the new product line and use the existing organization

A third alternative, rejecting the new line, was determined to be an inferior act early in the analysis and was eliminated from consideration.

The states of nature in this decision situation were defined in terms of 1,000-unit differentials of sales during the first year of marketing the new product. These states were:

s_1:   2,000 units
s_2:   3,000 units

s_3:   4,000 units
s_4:   5,000 units
s_5:   6,000 units
s_6:   7,000 units
s_7:   8,000 units

Probabilities were assigned to the individual states using the normal distribution, as described in Chapter 7. The probability distribution that Eastways management finally adopted is:

$$P(s_1) = .03$$
$$P(s_2) = .15$$
$$P(s_3) = .32$$
$$P(s_4) = .32$$
$$P(s_5) = .15$$
$$P(s_6) = .03$$
$$P(s_7) = 0$$

The Eastways decision situation is summarized in Figure 9.5, which is identical to Figure 4.8 with the state probabilities and the expected values added.

The expected values of the acts are computed as follows:

$EV(a_1)$ = $(.03)(-\$110,000) + (.15)(-\$40,000) + (.32)(\$30,000)$
$+ (.32)(\$100,000) + (.15)(\$170,000) + (.03)(\$240,000)$
$+ (0)(\$300,000)$
= \$65,000

$EV(a_2)$ = $(.03)(\$20,000) + (.15)(\$55,000) + (.32)(\$90,000)$
$+ (.32)(\$125,000) + (.15)(\$160,000) + (.03)(\$195,000)$
$+ (0)(\$230,000)$
= \$107,500

FIGURE 9.5   Payoff table for Eastways.

STATES	PROBABILITIES	ACTS	
		a_1	a_2
s_1	.03	−\$110,000	\$ 20,000
s_2	.15	−\$ 40,000	\$ 55,000
s_3	.32	\$ 30,000	\$ 90,000
s_4	.32	\$100,000	\$125,000
s_5	.15	\$170,000	\$160,000
s_6	.03	\$240,000	\$195,000
s_7	0	\$300,000	\$230,000
	1.00	EV \$ 65,000	\$107,500

Since the expected value of a_2 is greater than that of a_1, Eastways should handle the new product line using its existing organization.

The Thermocal Case

The Thermocal case originally involved a choice among three alternatives: developing and marketing a new solar power system, implementing an extensive advertising program, and maintaining the status quo. The last alternative was found to be inferior in the earlier analysis, reducing the viable alternatives to:

a_1:   develop and market the solar power system
a_2:   implement the advertising program

The states in this situation were defined as combinations of economic conditions and the presence or absence of competition. One state was found to be inconsequential and was eliminated. The remaining states are:

s_1:   economy good
s_2:   economy fair and no competition
s_3:   economy fair and competition
s_4:   economy poor and no competition
s_5:   economy poor and competition

Since these states cannot be represented by numerical values, the normal distribution cannot be used to assess their probabilities. Consequently, after several approximations using the betting-odds method, Thermocal's president arrived at the following probability distribution:

$$P(s_1) = .15$$
$$P(s_2) = .20$$
$$P(s_3) = .30$$
$$P(s_4) = .15$$
$$P(s_5) = .20$$

The decision situation is described in Figure 9.6, which is the same as Figure 4.10 with probabilities and expected values added.

FIGURE 9.6 Payoff table for Thermocal.

STATES	PROBABILITIES	ACTS	
		a_1	a_2
s_1	.15	$11 million	$8 million
s_2	.20	$ 7 million	$4 million
s_3	.30	$ 3 million	$4 million
s_4	.15	$ 0	$2 million
s_5	.20	−$ 1.5 million	$2 million
	1.00	EV $ 3.65 million	$3.9 million

The expected values of the acts are computed as follows:

$$
\begin{aligned}
EV(a_1) &= (.15)(\$11 \text{ million}) + (.20)(\$7 \text{ million}) + (.30)(\$3 \text{ million}) \\
&\quad + (.15)(0) + (.20)(-\$1.5 \text{ million}) \\
&= \$3.65 \text{ million}
\end{aligned}
$$

$$
\begin{aligned}
EV(a_2) &= (.15)(\$8 \text{ million}) + (.20)(\$4 \text{ million}) + (.30)(\$4 \text{ million}) \\
&\quad + (.15)(\$2 \text{ million}) + (.20)(\$2 \text{ million}) \\
&= \$3.9 \text{ million}
\end{aligned}
$$

In this case, the expected value of a_2 is greater than that of a_1. Consequently, under this criterion, a_2 is the better act. In other words, if all the conditional payoffs have been evaluated correctly and if the probability distribution truly reflects the decision maker's feelings about the likelihoods of the states, then Thermocal should implement the proposed advertising program instead of developing the solar power system.

THE EXPECTED VALUE CRITERION IN MULTISTAGE DECISION SITUATIONS

Whereas a single-stage decision situation requires but a single decision at one point in time, a multistage decision situation requires that two or more decisions be made at different points in time. Furthermore, although a single-stage decision situation can be completely described with a payoff table, this device is not suitable for describing a multistage situation. The best way to describe a multistage situation is by using a decision tree. (Decision trees can also be used to describe single-stage situations, but payoff tables are more convenient and easier to use in those cases.)

The application of the formal intuitive method becomes more complicated in multistage situations since these situations are inherently more complicated. In this section we will complete the formal intuitive process for all the multistage decision problems described in Chapter 6. The analysis in that chapter included the description of the situation with a decision tree and the pruning of the tree to eliminate inferior acts and inconsequential states. At this point we are ready to apply the expected value criterion. However, before we attempt this with a multistage problem, let's see how it works on a single-stage decision situation that is described with a decision tree.

The EDI Case

The EDI situation requires that a decision be made either to bid at one of three price levels or not to bid. The payoff table for this situation is shown in Figure 9.2. A decision tree description of the same problem is provided in Figure 9.7. (This is Figure 6.6 with additional information added.)

As Figure 9.7 shows, at the first and only decision node the decision maker must choose from among four acts: a_1, a_2, a_3, and a_4. These acts are represented by the four branches issuing from that node. Each of these branches leads to a chance node and each of the chance nodes has four branches which correspond to the four possible states of nature: s_1, s_2, s_3, and s_4. The probability assigned to each state is noted on the appropriate branch. At the end of each branch is the conditional payoff which corresponds to that particular sequence of act and state. That is, a_1 and s_3 result in a conditional payoff of $-\$95,000$; a_3 and s_2 result in a conditional payoff of $\$125,000$; and so on.

The expected value of each act is computed in exactly the same way it was done earlier in the chapter. That is, each conditional payoff is multiplied by the probability of the corresponding state, and the products are added for all the states. For example:

$$
\begin{aligned}
EV(a_1) &= (.05)(\$475,000) + (.15)(-\$95,000) + (.35)(-\$95,000) \\
&\quad + (.45)(-\$95,000) \\
&= -\$66,500
\end{aligned}
$$

$$EV(a_2) = (.05)(\$350,000) + (.15)(\$350,000) + (.35)(-\$95,000)$$
$$+ (.45)(-\$95,000)$$
$$= -6,000$$

$$EV(a_3) = (.05)(\$125,000) + (.15)(\$125,000) + (.35)(\$125,000)$$
$$+ (.45)(-\$95,000)$$
$$= \$26,000$$

$$EV(a_4) = (.05)(0) + (.15)(0) + (.35)(0) + (.45)(0)$$
$$= 0$$

FIGURE 9.7 Complete decision tree for modified EDI bid decision.

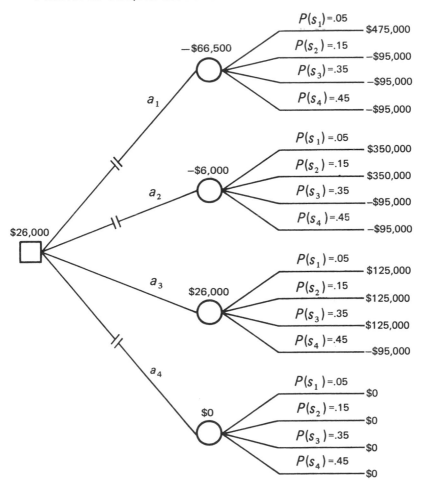

Notice that the expected value of each act is written on the decision tree directly above the chance node at the end of each of the act branches.

Now consider the decision maker standing at the decision node. At the end of each branch corresponding to an available act he sees the expected value of the act. Seeking to maximize his expected gain, he compares the expected values and selects the act for which the expected payoff is the greatest. In this situation, that act is a_3. He completes the decision tree analysis by blocking off each of the inferior acts with a double line.

A multistage decision problem is analyzed in exactly the same way except that the procedure must be applied at each stage in the problem. Beginning with the expected payoffs at the extreme right side of the decision tree, the decision maker works from right to left until he can place a single expected value at the decision node on the extreme left.

The Granger Case—
The First Multistage Situation

The Granger case was first discussed in Chapter 4 as a single-stage decision situation. Then, in Chapter 6, certain complications were added to convert it to a multistage problem. The first of these complications was to provide Granger with the option of postponing his decision on Southeastern Mutual's offer until June 1. However, the cost of exercising this option is $100,000. That is, the price offered for Granger's 25 acres is $600,000 if Granger accepts by April 1 but only $500,000 if Granger waits until June 1 to accept.

If Granger rejects Southeastern's offer, he may be able to sell the land for $750,000 if an expressway route across his land is approved by the state highway department. The state will make that decision on May 31. If the expressway route is not approved and Granger rejects Southeastern's offer, he can still sell the land as building lots for $475,000.

A decision tree describing this situation is shown in Figure 9.8. With inferior acts eliminated, the tree is reduced to the one shown in Figure 9.9. (This is Figure 6.14 with some additional

information added.) The process of pruning the tree has simplified the description of this multistage decision situation significantly, as we can see by comparing Figure 9.8 with Figure 9.9.
However, the decision maker must still choose between accepting
the offer immediately and postponing his decision until June 1.

The states in this situation correspond to the approval or
nonapproval of the expressway route. Granger assessed these
probabilities subjectively using the betting-odds method and arrived at the following values:

$$P(\text{route approved}) \quad = .35$$
$$P(\text{route not approved}) = .65$$

These probabilities are noted at the appropriate branches of the
tree in Figure 9.9.

In analyzing the tree, we begin with the payoffs at the extreme right of the diagram and work from top to bottom. The
first payoff is $600,000, at the end of the "accept" branch. Since
there are no chance or decision nodes between this payoff and
the initial decision node at 4/1/80, we simply move on to the next
payoff.

The payoff just below $600,000 is $750,000, at the end of the
"reject" branch issuing from the decision node of 6/1/80. Since
there are no other branches issuing from that node and no
intervening chance nodes, the $750,000 payoff is moved to the
left and written above that decision node. The next payoff is
$500,000, at the end of the "accept" branch issuing from the
decision node at 6/1/80. Again, we simply move that payoff to
the left and write it above the appropriate decision node.

Moving to the left on the diagram, we encounter a chance
node at 5/31/80. On this date the expressway decision will be
made by the state highway department. Issuing from this node
are the two states that correspond to the possible results of that
decision. The probabilities assigned to the two states are noted
on the branches. If the route is approved, the better act is
"reject," with a payoff of $750,000. If the route is not approved,
the better act is "accept," with a payoff of $500,000. At the
chance node of 5/31/80 we can evaluate the expected value of the
act "postpone" issuing from the initial decision node of 4/1/80.

That expected value is $750,000 with a probability of .35 and $500,000 with a probability of .65. Therefore:

$$EV(\text{postpone}) = (.35)(\$750,000) + (.65)(\$500,000)$$
$$= \$262,500 + \$325,000$$
$$= \$587,500$$

This value is written above the chance node of 5/31/80.

At the initial decision node of 4/1/80, Granger must decide whether to accept Southeastern Mutual's offer immediately or postpone his decision until June 1, by which time the status of the expressway route will be known. Looking down the two branches, he sees a value of $600,000 at the end of the "accept"

FIGURE 9.8 Decision tree for Granger case with option to postpone.

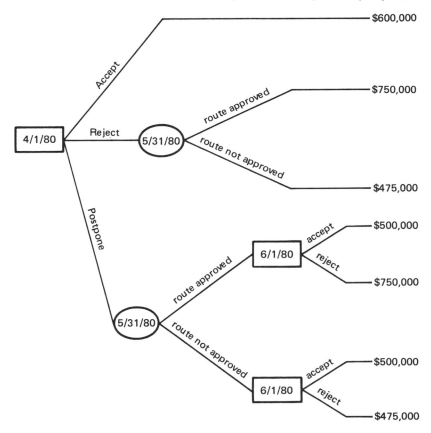

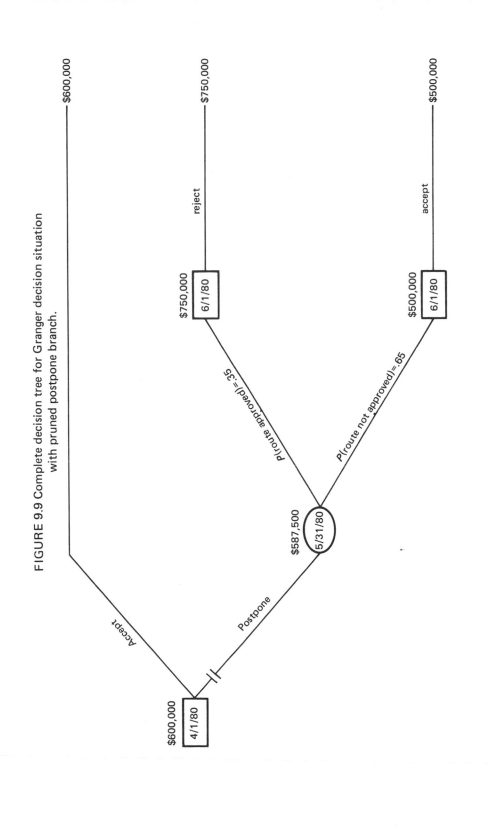

FIGURE 9.9 Complete decision tree for Granger decision situation with pruned postpone branch.

branch and an expected value of $587,500 at the end of the "postpone" branch. Since a decision maker should select the act with the highest actual or expected value, Granger should block off the "postpone" branch with a double line and accept the offer.

The Granger Case—
Additional Complications

An additional complication to the Granger case resulted from the information that the Tristate Development Company is considering developing a new shopping mall on 100 acres of land adjacent to Granger's property. If the mall is built, it would increase the value of Granger's land as a residential development. Under those circumstances, Granger estimates that his profit on the sale of the land as building lots would increase from $475,000 to $525,000. However, Tristate will not make its decision on the mall until July 1. A new decision tree for the complete Granger decision situation is provided in Figure 9.10. (This is Figure 6.15 with additional information added.)

There are now two new states of nature in the decision situation. The probabilities of the original two states, "route approved" and "route not approved," were assessed at .35 and .65 respectively. The probabilities of the two new states, "mall" and "no mall," were assessed by the betting-odds method as .90 and .10 respectively. These probabilities have been inserted on the appropriate state branches of the decision tree in Figure 9.10.

In this case we must begin the analysis with the payoffs issuing from nodes with the most recent dates and work backward, from right to left, toward the earliest dates. The nodes containing the most recent dates are the chance nodes dated 7/1. Beginning with the topmost, we find conditional consequences of $525,000 and $475,000 at the end of the state branches issuing from that node. The expected value or payoff at that chance node is calculated in the same way as the expected value of an act. That is, we multiply each conditional payoff by the state probability on the branch leading to that payoff and add these

FIGURE 9.10 Complete Granger decision problem.

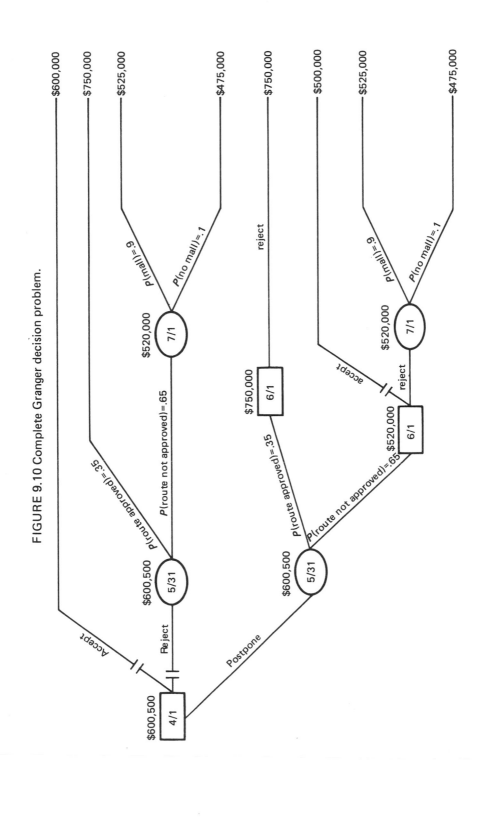

products. In this case, we have $525,000 with a probability of .90 and $475,000 with a probability of .10. Therefore, the expected payoff at this chance node is (.90)($525,000) + (.10)($475,000) = $520,000. This value is written above the node dated 7/1.

Proceeding downward, we find another chance node dated 7/1 with the same branches and payoffs as the one above. Consequently, the expected payoff at that node is also $520,000.

As we move to the left, the next nodes are decision nodes dated 6/1. Looking at the topmost node, we find a single "reject" branch leading to a payoff of $750,000. Since there is only one branch and no intervening nodes, the value of $750,000 is moved to the left and written above that node. At the second 6/1 decision node there are two branches: "accept" and "reject." There is a payoff of $500,000 at the end of the "accept" branch and an expected payoff of $520,000 above the chance node at the end of the "reject" branch. Since $520,000 is greater than $500,000, the "accept" branch is blocked off with a double line and the value $520,000 is written above that 6/1 decision node.

Again moving from right to left, we encounter two chance nodes dated 5/31. Looking at the topmost node first, we see two state branches leading to payoffs or expected payoffs of $750,-000 and $520,000 with probabilities of .35 and .65 respectively. This indicates that if the expressway route is approved there is a payoff of $750,000, but if it is not approved there is an expected payoff of $520,000. The uncertainty about those states is represented by their probabilities. The expected payoff at the topmost 5/31 chance node is then (.35)($750,000) + (.65)($520,000) = $600,500. The value $600,500 is written above that chance node and represents the expected value of the act "reject" issuing from the initial decision node at 4/1.

At the next chance node dated 5/31, the same conditions exist. The expected value at that node is also $600,500; this value is written directly above the node. Since this node is at the end of the "postpone" branch issuing from the initial decision node dated 4/1, the $600,500 represents the expected value of the act "postpone."

The next node to consider is the initial decision node at 4/1. At this node the decision maker can look down a branch corresponding to each of the acts available to him. At the end of the "accept" branch he sees a payoff of $600,000. At the end of the "reject" and "postpone" branches he sees expected payoffs of $600,500. Since $600,000 is less than $600,500, the "accept" decision is clearly inferior and that branch is blocked off. However, the expected payoffs at the ends of the other two branches are exactly the same. Which of these two should the decision maker choose?

The "reject" branch represents an immediate rejection of Southeastern Mutual's offer on 4/1. The "postpone" branch allows the decision maker to delay his response to the offer for two months, until 6/1. In either case the expected payoff is the same. However, an immediate rejection is irrevocable. A decision to postpone provides the decision maker with an additional two months, during which time additional information might become available to change the decision situation. Since time itself has value, and in this case costs the decision maker nothing, he should select the "postpone" alternative and block off the "reject" branch. If no additional information pertinent to the decision situation is forthcoming in the next two months, Granger should reject Southeastern Mutual's offer on 6/1.

The Thermocal Case

The complete decision tree for the Thermocal case is given in Figure 9.11. (This is Figure 6.20 with additional information added.)

The Thermocal case was initially presented as a single-stage decision situation. Then a complication was added that converted it to a multistage situation and necessitated an adjustment to the state probabilities originally assigned. In the single-stage Thermocal problem, two sets of factors relating to the condition of the economy and the presence or absence of competition were combined into a single set of states. Since both factors were unresolved at the time that the single decision had to be made, this combination was permissible. In the multistage Thermocal situation, however, there are two decision dates. The second decision date follows the resolution date for the economic factor

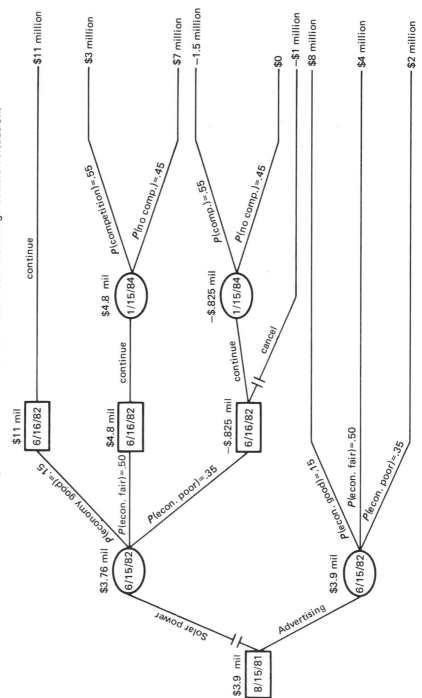

FIGURE 9.11 Complete decision tree for final Thermocal multistage decision situation.

but precedes the resolution date for the competition factor. Under these circumstances, the two sets of states must be considered separately and probabilities assigned to each set.

There is a rule of probability which states that if two events are independent of one another, the probability that they both occur is equal to the product of their individual probabilities. Thermocal's president had previously assigned probabilities to states that combined two events, such as "economy fair and no competition" and "economy poor and competition." He must now assign probabilities separately to the set of economic conditions and the set representing the state of the competition. In doing so, he should be sure that his assessment of the individual state probabilities is consistent with his original assessment of the probability assigned to the combined states. For example, the probability he assigns to the state "economy fair" multiplied by the probability of the state "no competition" should be approximately equal to the probability he originally assigned to the state "economy fair and no competition."

Suppose that, using the betting-odds procedure, the president of Thermocal arrives at the following assessments of the two sets of independent states of nature:

> *Economy*
> P(economy good) = .15
> P(economy fair) = .50
> P(economy poor) = .35
>
> *Competition*
> P(no competition) = .45
> P(competition) = .55

Checking these probabilities against those assigned to the combined states previously, we would get the products shown in Table 9.1. Note that the probabilities resulting from the multiplication of the individual factors agree quite closely with those assigned to the states consisting of the combined factors. If large discrepancies had occurred between the two sets, Thermocal's president would have had to reassess all the state probabilities to account for the differences.

The two different sets of state probabilities are shown on the

TABLE 9.1   Product of separate state probabilities.

Combined States	Probability
Economy good	.15
Economy fair, no competition	.20
Economy fair, competition	.30
Economy poor, no competition	.15
Economy poor, competition	.20
	1.00

Product of Separate State Probabilities				
P(econ. good)				.15
P(econ. fair)	$\times$ P(no comp.)	=	(.50)(.45) =	.23
P(econ. fair)	$\times$ P(comp.)	=	(.50)(.55) =	.28
P(econ. poor)	$\times$ P(no comp.)	=	(.35)(.45) =	.16
P(econ. poor)	$\times$ P(comp.)	=	(.35)(.55) =	.19
				1.00

decision tree in Figure 9.11. Notice that the state branches which relate to economic conditions issue from the chance nodes dated 6/15/82. The state branches which relate to the competition issue from the chance nodes dated 1/15/84.

To analyze the decision tree, we begin with the nodes having the most recent date. The first nodes to be considered are the two chance nodes with resolution dates of 1/15/84. The topmost of these nodes has two branches leading to payoffs of $3 million and $7 million with probabilities of .55 and .45 respectively. The expected payoff at that node is computed to be $4.8 million. The second chance node dated 1/15/84 has two branches leading to payoffs of −$1.5 million (that is, a loss of $1.5 million) and $0 with probabilities of .55 and .45 respectively. The expected payoff at that node is −$.825 million, or −$825,000.

As we move to the left of the diagram, the next most recent date is 6/16/82, which is associated with three decision nodes. Starting with the topmost of these nodes, we see that a "continue" branch issues from the node and results in a payoff of $11 million. Since there are no other branches or intervening nodes, the payoff of $11 million can be written directly over that decision node. The next decision node dated 6/16/82 also has a single "continue" branch. This branch leads to an expected payoff of $4.8 million, and that value can be written above the node. The remaining decision node dated 6/16/82 has a "continue" branch leading to an expected payoff of $-\$.825$ million and a "cancel" branch leading to a payoff of $-\$1$ million. Since a loss of \$825,000 is to be preferred to a loss of \$1 million, the "cancel" branch is blocked off with a double line and the expected payoff of $-\$.825$ million is written above the node.

Again moving to the left, we encounter two chance nodes at 6/15/82. The topmost of these nodes has three branches leading to payoffs of \$11 million, \$4.8 million, and $-\$.825$ million with probabilities of .15, .50, and .35 respectively. The expected payoff is computed from the three conditional payoffs and their probabilities. The computed value, \$3.76 million, is written above the node. The lower chance node at 6/15/82 has three branches leading to payoffs of \$8 million, \$4 million, and \$2 million with probabilities of .15, .50, and .35 respectively. The expected payoff of \$3.9 million is computed and written above that node.

Now the decision maker, standing at the initial decision node dated 8/15/81, can look down the "solar power system" branch and see an expected payoff of \$3.76 million. Looking down the "advertising" branch, he can see an expected payoff of \$3.9 million. Since \$3.9 million is greater than \$3.76 million, the solar power system branch is blocked off and the optimal decision is to implement the advertising program.

SUMMARY OF THE PROCEDURES
FOR EVALUATING DECISION TREES

In approaching any decision situation, the decision maker can eliminate many complexities by accurately describing the situation and then eliminating inferior acts and inconsequential states. This procedure is referred to as "pruning" the decision tree. Once the decision tree has been simplified as much as possible, the state probabilities should be assessed and the tree evaluated. This is accomplished in the following manner:

1. Enter each state probability on the branch of the decision tree which corresponds to that state of nature.
2. Working from right to left—that is, from the most recent

dates to the earliest dates—assign a payoff or expected payoff to every node and write the value above the node. When a single branch issues from a node, the payoff at the end of that branch should be moved to the left and written above the node.

3. In evaluating a chance node with two or more branches, compute the expected payoff and write it above the node.

4. In evaluating a decision node with two or more branches, assign the larger of the payoffs or expected payoffs at the end of the branches to the decision node and block off the branches leading to the other payoffs.

5. Continue this procedure until a payoff is obtained for the initial decision node and all branches leading from the initial node are blocked except one.

SENSITIVITY OF RESULTS TO THE PROBABILITY ASSESSMENTS

In our discussion of subjective probability assessments, we mentioned that the choice of an optimal act using the expected value criterion and the formal intuitive method is relatively insensitive to small changes in the probabilities assigned to the states of nature. This can be demonstrated easily for decision situations that involve two alternative acts and two states of nature.

For two-act, two-state problems, it is possible to determine an indifference or breakeven value of the probability of one of the states simply by equating the expected values of the two acts and solving for a probability value. For example, in the single-stage Granger case, there were two states of nature:

s_1: expressway route approved
s_2: expressway route not approved

The probability of s_1 was assessed as .35. The probability of s_2 is simply $1 - P(s_1) = 1 - .35 = .65$.

The acts in the decision situation were:

a_1: accept offer
a_2: reject offer

The conditional payoff for a_1 was \$600,000 regardless of the state of nature. The payoffs for a_2 were \$750,000 if s_1 and \$475,000 if s_2.

If we write the formulas for the expected value of each act and insert the conditional payoffs, we get:

$$EV(a_1) = P(s_1)(\$600,000) + 1 - P(s_1)(\$600,000)$$
$$EV(a_2) = P(s_1)(\$750,000) + 1 - P(s_1)(\$475,000)$$

Now, if we equate $EV(a_1)$ and $EV(a_2)$ by letting the right side of the first equation equal the right side of the second and then solve for the value of $P(s_1)$, we obtain a probability that makes the expected values of both acts equal. This is called an *indifference value*, since the selection of either act will have exactly the same result. However, one act will be optimal for any probability below the indifference value, and the other act will be optimal for any probability greater than the indifference value.

Solving for the indifference value of $P(s_1)$ in the single-stage Granger case, we get $P(s_1) = .4545$. If the probability that the expressway route is approved is exactly .4545, then both acts have the same expected value and neither is an optimal act. In other words, Granger could choose either act and have exactly the same expectations. However, if the probability of route approval is any value less than .4545, acceptance of the offer is the optimal act. Conversely, if the probability is any value greater than .4545, rejection is the optimal act.

In assessing this probability, Granger arrived at .35 for $P(s_1)$. However, if his subjective probability for that state had been .45 or .40 or .25, his decision would have been exactly the same. In multistate and multiaction problems, the leeway in assessing probabilities is not as great as it is in two-state, two-action problems. However, even in those cases, small differences in state probabilities should have little effect on the outcome. In assessing probabilities, then, the decision maker should not worry about being accurate to plus or minus a percentage point. Instead, he should be more concerned that his final probability distribution truly reflects his subjective feelings.

10

ADDITIONAL TOOLS
FOR INTUITIVE DECISION MAKERS

By this time, the reader should be aware of the importance of the proper interpretation of observed information in the decision-making process. The previous chapters have been devoted to describing various methods of analyzing and using data in the formal intuitive decision-making procedure. Many of these methods were approximate and depended greatly on the concept of subjective probability and on the assumption of normal distributions. The common factor among these techniques was that they were commonsense procedures that utilized the informed judgment of the decision maker. Even more important, they were practical and easy to apply. In this chapter we will discuss several other techniques that also meet the criteria of common sense and ease of application. These techniques provide information that the decision maker can use to form judgments about such factors as relationships, trends, and objectivity.

TESTING FOR ASSOCIATION

Relationships among different factors are common in everyday life. It is easy to find examples of such associations. For instance, people's heights and weights are certainly related. Perhaps the relationship isn't perfect, but taller people tend to weigh more than shorter people. Of course this does not preclude the existence of short heavy people or tall thin ones, but in general the relationship holds true. It isn't difficult to find evidence that earning capacity and education are related. In general, more education means higher earnings. Again, this may not be true in every case, but then perfect relationships are rare and should not be expected.

Relationships between different factors are also common in business. It isn't difficult to see that there is an association between sales and advertising expenditures, housing starts and birth rates, productivity and length of shift, and so on. Intuitive business decision makers are keen observers of the business environment and, like detectives, find clues to such relationships by observing the movements of various factors in their environment. When two factors, call them X and Y, appear to move in concert consistently, this information can be useful in making decisions. Or, if X and Y move in opposite directions, this too can be helpful in drawing conclusions and making decisions. When two factors are related such that the movement of one coincides with some movement in the other, the factors are said to be correlated. If X and Y move in the same direction, they are positively correlated. If they move in opposite directions, they are negatively correlated.

Of course, such correlations are seldom perfect. In other words, even though X and Y are correlated, Y will not always change by exactly the same amount for a given change in X. Nevertheless, knowledge about such a correlation is a valuable decision-making tool. Consequently, it can be very helpful for a decision maker to be able to determine when such a relationship exists, assess whether it is positive or negative, and then compute some numerical value that measures the strength of the correlation.

Statisticians have developed techniques for measuring and using such correlations. These techniques are called correlation and regression analysis. However, as with other statistical techniques, they can require an extensive knowledge of mathematics and statistics and can be time-consuming and difficult to apply. In this chapter we will introduce a few simple methods that accomplish many of the same things as the more complicated procedures.

Consider a situation in which the personnel manager of a large manufacturing firm has been administering aptitude tests to applicants for a particular position. Since administration of the tests costs money, in order for the test to be worthwhile it should assist the manager in selecting applicants who will perform well on the job. In other words, there should be some relationship between the test score and job performance.

In gathering information to use in deciding whether to continue testing, the manager obtains the records of ten employees selected at random from the personnel files. Each file includes a record of the employee's score on the aptitude test as well as a production efficiency rating which is computed monthly on each employee for evaluation purposes. The manager has an assistant list both scores for each employee, as shown in Table 10.1.

It is difficult to conclude anything about a possible relationship between the two factors just from looking at the numbers in the table. However, there is a simple method for displaying the data, which tends to show the presence or absence of a relationship more clearly. Such a display is called a *scatter diagram.*

A scatter diagram is constructed by drawing two perpendicular lines or axes on a piece of paper, preferably graph paper. The horizontal axis is labeled X and is scaled in the units in

TABLE 10.1   Employee ratings.

Employee	Aptitude Test Score X	Production Efficiency Score Y
1	80	70
2	80	60
3	45	24
4	70	38
5	95	45
6	20	30
7	50	35
8	90	50
9	25	25
10	50	20

which X is observed. The vertical axis is labeled Y and is similarly scaled in appropriate units. Then a point is marked on the graph for each pair of observed X,Y values. For example, in this case employee 1 had an X score of 80 and a Y score of 70. A point is marked on the graph corresponding to $X = 80$ and $Y = 70$. Employee 2 had an X score of 80 and a Y score of 60. Another point is marked on the graph at the intersection of these two values. The process is continued for all ten employees.

The scatter diagram that results from this procedure is shown in Figure 10.1. Notice that the points seem to distribute themselves in a pattern running from the lower left-hand corner of the graph to the upper right-hand corner. In fact, it appears as

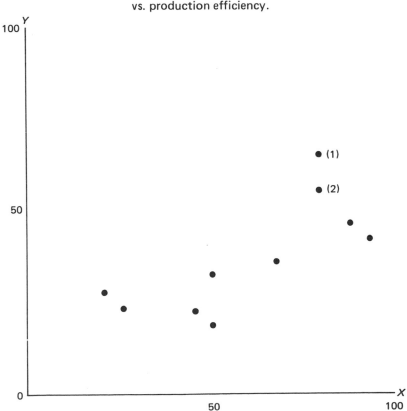

FIGURE 10.1 Scatter diagram of aptitude test scores vs. production efficiency.

though large values of X go with large values of Y and small values of X with small values of Y. It would not be too hard to visualize a straight line slanting from the lower left to the upper right about which the points tend to cluster. Such a pattern is evidence of a positive correlation between the two variables and might indicate that, with some exceptions, applicants who score high on the aptitude test tend to have high production efficiency scores and vice versa.

On the other hand, if a scatter diagram looked like Figure 10.2, which is not the case in our example, we might visualize a line running from the upper left to the lower right—evidence of a negative correlation between the two factors.

A third pattern that might occur is a rather uniform distribution of the points across the diagram, as shown in Figure 10.3. Such a pattern does not suggest any sort of line and is evidence of no correlation between the two factors. When this type of pattern, or lack of it, occurs, the decision maker might conclude that since there appears to be no relationship between the two factors, little information about one can be obtained by observing the other. In the case of the test scores and production efficiency, if a pattern of no correlation appeared on the scatter diagram the personnel manager would have a reasonable basis for discontinuing the aptitude test, since it appears to be unrelated to job performance.

Let's get back to the scatter diagram in Figure 10.1. Drawing the diagram—scaling the two axes and plotting the points—is not difficult, particularly when there are only ten pairs of values. However, if there were 30 or 50 points to plot, it might be a time-consuming and tedious task. Since we want to use tools that are as simple as possible, we might try to determine what would happen if we plotted *ranks* of the observations instead of the observed values themselves. By ranks we mean that the largest value gets a 1, the second largest value a 2, and so on. Table 10.2 shows the original data with ranks assigned to the values of each factor. Notice that ties receive the average of their ranks. For example, an X score of 80 occupies ranks 3 and 4. Therefore each value of 80 gets the rank 3.5.

If the ten pairs of ranks are plotted on a scatter diagram, the X and Y axes need only be scaled in equal intervals from 1 to 10.

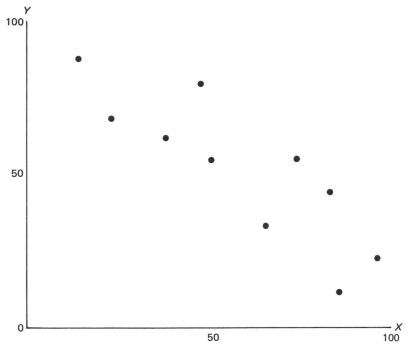

FIGURE 10.2 Scatter diagram showing negative correlation.

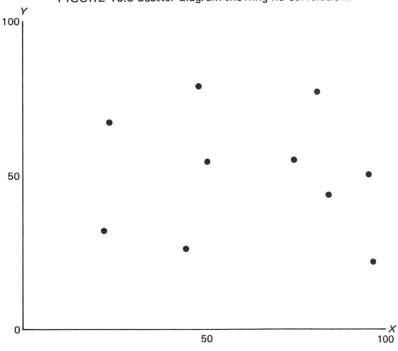

FIGURE 10.3 Scatter diagram showing no correlation.

TABLE 10.2 Data on aptitude test scores
and production efficiency, with ranks.

Employee	Aptitude Test Score X	Rank of X	Production Efficiency Score Y	Rank of Y
1	80	3.5	70	1
2	80	3.5	60	2
3	45	8	24	9
4	70	5	38	5
5	95	1	45	4
6	20	10	30	7
7	50	6.5	35	6
8	90	2	50	3
9	25	9	25	8
10	50	6.5	20	10

The scatter diagram of ranks is shown in Figure 10.4. Notice that this diagram is very similar to Figure 10.1. In fact, it is difficult to tell the difference between the two, and the pattern is just as evident using ranks as it is using the actual scores. High ranks of X tend to be associated with high ranks of Y and low ranks of X with low ranks of Y. We might conclude that it is much easier to construct a scatter diagram on the basis of ranks than on actual scores and that the information obtained from such a diagram is just as good. In this case, the decision maker might conclude from either Figure 10.1 or Figure 10.4 that the aptitude test scores are related to future job performance, and he might continue using the test as a screening tool in hiring.

A MEASURE OF CORRELATION

A decision maker is not always able to judge whether a correlation exists between two factors simply by observing a pattern of points on a graph. A reference line that appears to best fit the pattern of points would aid the decision maker's judgment. If the points tend to cluster closely about the line—a good fit—this is an indication of a strong correlation between the two factors. The greater the divergence of the points from the line, the weaker the correlation.

The reference line could be drawn solely on the basis of the decision maker's judgment, or by one of several curve-fitting methods. In many instances the subjectively drawn line is adequate. However, if we want a line that can be duplicated by anyone from the same set of data, we should use an objective method. The semiaverage method provides a very easy way of fitting a line to a set of points.

The semiaverage method is simple, requires very little calculation, and can be done quickly. The data are divided into two parts, a lower half and an upper half, according to the X ranks. If there are an even number of pairs of data, as in the example we have been using, the data are divided exactly in half. In other words, the X ranks 1 through 5 are in one half and the X ranks 6 through 10 are in the other. If there are an odd number of pairs

FIGURE 10.4 Scatter diagram of ranks of aptitude test scores and production efficiency scores.

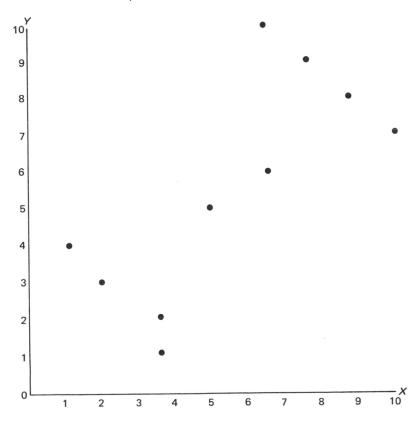

of data, the middle pair can simply be eliminated for this procedure. Then the Y ranks corresponding to the X ranks in each
respective half are averaged. The average of each half is plotted
directly above a value on the X scale that falls midway between
the ranks averaged. In our example, the average of the lower
half would be plotted above the point on the X scale corresponding to 2.5 and the average of the upper half would be plotted
above the point on the X scale corresponding to 7.5. A line is
drawn connecting these two points. The calculations for the
example are shown in Table 10.3, and the semiaverage line is
shown in Figure 10.5. The two semiaverages are:

$$\bar{Y}_1 = \frac{15}{5} = 3$$

$$\bar{Y}_2 = \frac{40}{5} = 8$$

Once the line is plotted, we can get a much better picture of the
way the points are distributed about the line. If every point falls
exactly on the line, we would have a perfect correlation. This
condition is extremely unlikely. A very wide scatter about the
line indicates a very weak relationship or no relationship at all.
Again, the interpretation of the scatter about the line is very
subjective. The scatter in Figure 10.5 indicates a moderately
strong correlation between the aptitude test scores and the production efficiency scores. Figures 10.6 and 10.7 illustrate *very
strong* and *very weak* patterns of correlation respectively.

On observing these diagrams, an effective manager might
logically ask: How strong or how weak is the correlation between

TABLE 10.3 Data for plotting semiaverage line.

Lowest Half of X Ranks	Corresponding Y Rank	Highest Half of X Ranks	Corresponding Y Rank
1	4	6.5	6
2	3	6.5	10
3.5	1	8	9
3.5	2	9	8
5	5	10	7
	15		40

FIGURE 10.5 Scatter diagram with semiaverage line.

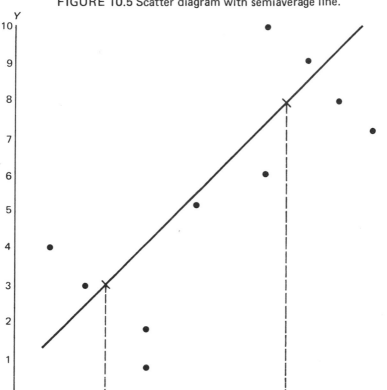

the two factors? Is it possible to measure the correlation and express it numerically? The answer to this second question is yes, correlation can be measured numerically. There is a value called the *product moment correlation coefficient* which does just that. This measure is somewhat complicated and can be time-consuming to compute. However, there is another measure of correlation based only on ranks that is very easy to compute. It is called the *coefficient of rank correlation* and is defined as follows:

$$r = 1 - \frac{6 \, \Sigma(X_r - Y_r)^2}{n(n^2 - 1)}$$

where r stands for the correlation coefficient, X_r and Y_r stand for the ranks of the corresponding X and Y values respectively, and

FIGURE 10.6 Scatter diagram illustrating strong correlation.

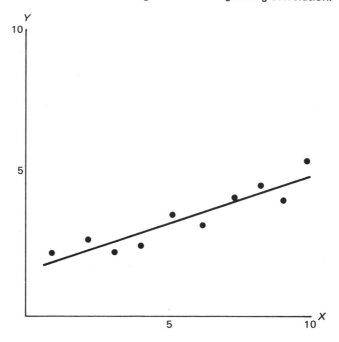

FIGURE 10.7 Scatter diagram illustrating weak correlation.

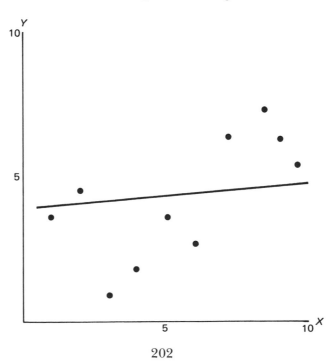

n represents the number of pairs of ranks observed. (Σ is the summation symbol and means add up whatever follows.)

Application of this formula will result in a number between 0 and 1, where 0 indicates that there is no correlation between the factors and 1 represents a perfect correlation. The sign, plus or minus, tells whether the correlation is positive or negative—that is, direct or inverse. For the data in the example, the computation of r is illustrated in Table 10.4.

A correlation coefficient of approximately .75 on a scale of 0 to 1 is a moderately strong correlation and provides the manager in our example with a basis for deciding whether to continue to administer the aptitude tests. Of course, the manager must still exercise his judgment in the matter, since it is not possible to establish a firm set of rules on what values of r constitute a strong enough correlation to act in some particular manner and what values do not. If a rough guideline is required, we might adopt the rule that a correlation coefficient of .5 or less, positive or negative, indicates a relatively weak relationship.

To gain a better idea about the relationship of scatter and the coefficient of correlation, we can look at some other diagrams. The data resulting in the scatter diagram of Figure 10.7 have a

TABLE 10.4 Computation of rank correlation coefficient for aptitude test and production efficiency scores.

Employee	Rank of X	Rank of Y	$X_r - Y_r$	$(X_r - Y_r)^2$
1	3.5	1	2.5	6.25
2	3.5	2	1.5	2.25
3	8	9	-1.0	1.00
4	5	5	0	0
5	1	4	-3.0	9.00
6	10	7	3.0	9.00
7	6.5	6	0.5	0.25
8	2	3	-1.0	1.00
9	9	8	1.0	1.00
10	6.5	10	-3.5	12.25
				42.00

$$r = 1 - \frac{6\Sigma(X_r - Y_r)^2}{n(n^2 - 1)} = 1 - \frac{(6)(42)}{(10)(100 - 1)}$$

$$= 1 - \frac{252}{990} = 1 - .255 = .745$$

coefficient of correlation of about .47. The data resulting in the scatter diagram of Figure 10.6 have a coefficient of correlation of about .94.

One final point. How much accuracy or information do we sacrifice when we discard the original numerical observations and use only ranks in our calculations? If the actual numerical values are used to compute the correlation coefficient (product moment coefficient) for the same data, the resulting value is approximately .73, a figure that is very close to the value .75 computed from the ranks only.

TESTING FOR TREND

Business executives frequently look for trends to help them make decisions. A trend is a relationship between two factors, one of which is time. In the test for association discussed above, if the X factor is time—that is, the time at which a value of the Y factor is observed—then a relationship between the Y factor and time is called a trend. Under those circumstances, the test for association becomes a test for trend.

The test for trend involves determining whether changes in some factor occur consistently over time. For example, labor and material costs and consumer prices seem to increase consistently year after year. However, trends can apply to other than economic factors. Consider the case of a production manager who is concerned about the proportion of defective products coming off his production lines. The manager has to decide whether to use overtime to produce a precision electronic component for which the delivery date is fast approaching. This decision might be based, at least in part, on the change in the proportion of defective products produced as the length of the shift increases. Suppose that a record is kept of the proportion of defectives produced during each of the eight hours. We will represent this proportion with the letter Y. The X factor is simply time—that is, each value of X corresponds to the hours 1 through 8 of the shift. The values of X are actually ranks—the first hour, the second hour, and so on. The values of Y, the proportion of defective product observed each hour, can be ranked from smallest to largest. That is, the rank 1 is assigned to the smallest value of the proportion, the rank 2 to the next smallest, and so on. The data are shown in Table 10.5.

A scatter diagram for these data can be constructed using the ranks of X and Y in exactly the same way as before. This scatter diagram appears in Figure 10.8, with the semiaverage line drawn in. The semiaverages are plotted above the X values of 2 and 6 and the line is drawn between the two points. The computation of the semiaverages is shown in Table 10.6.

The scatter diagram in Figure 10.8 suggests that a trend does exist. There appears to be a consistent increase in the proportion

FIGURE 10.8 Scatter diagram of ranks: proportion of defective products and length of shift.

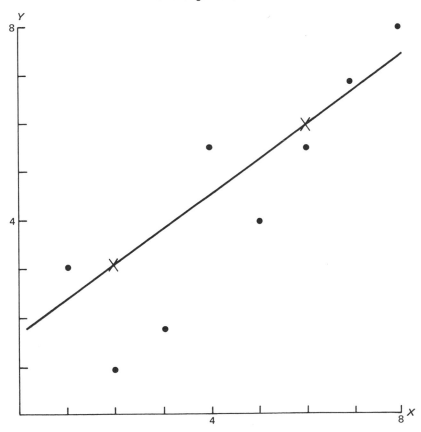

TABLE 10.5   Data on proportion of defective product.

Hour X	Proportion Defective Y	Rank of Y
1	.08	3
2	.05	1
3	.07	2
4	.10	5.5
5	.09	4
6	.10	5.5
7	.11	7
8	.13	8

TABLE 10.6   Computation of semiaverages.

Lowest Half of X Ranks	Corresponding Y Rank	Highest Half of X Ranks	Corresponding Y Rank
1	3	5	4
2	1	6	5.5
3	2	7	7
4	5.5	8	8
	11.5		24.5

$$\bar{Y}_1 = \frac{11.5}{4} = 2.9 \qquad \bar{Y}_2 = \frac{24.5}{4} = 6.1$$

TABLE 10.7   Computation of rank correlation coefficient for proportion of defective product over time.

Hour	Rank of X	Rank of Y	$X_r - Y_r$	$(X_r - Y_r)^2$
1	1	3	-2.0	4.00
2	2	1	1.0	1.00
3	3	2	1.0	1.00
4	4	5.5	-1.5	2.25
5	5	4	1.0	1.00
6	6	5.5	1.5	2.25
7	7	7	0	0
8	8	8	0	0
				11.50

$$r = 1 - \frac{6\Sigma(X_r - Y_r)^2}{n(n^2 - 1)} = 1 - \frac{(6)(11.50)}{(64)(7)}$$

$$= 1 - \frac{69}{448} = 1 - .154 = .846$$

of defective product produced as the shift progresses. Also, the points seem to cluster fairly closely about the line. The numerical measure of the strength of the relationship between the Y factor and time can be computed just as it was in the previous section. The computation of the correlation coefficient is shown in Table 10.7.

An r value of approximately .85 is a reasonably high correlation and indicates the existence of a fairly strong trend. Since the proportion of defective product appears to increase with time, the production manager might consider it inadvisable to lengthen the shift with overtime.

As another example, consider a marketing executive faced with a decision about entering a new product market. The manager might be concerned about whether the demand for the product has been increasing with time. Data on the sale of the product were collected for a 15-year period and adjusted for the effect of inflation. The data are presented in Table 10.8. X represents the year and Y represents sales in millions of dollars.

A scatter diagram for these data is shown in Figure 10.9, with the semiaverage line drawn in. If any trend does exist in the data, it is apparently a negative one—that is, sales appear to be decreasing with time. In the absence of a positive trend, and basing his judgment solely on the scatter diagram, the marketing executive might conclude that conditions are not favorable for entering the new market. If he needs additional information before making a final decision, he might compute the correlation coefficient from the data. The computations are shown in Table 10.9.

The correlation coefficient verifies that the relationship between time and sales in this case is negative. The coefficient of about .65 does not indicate a particularly strong relationship, but coupled with the fact that it is negative, it should convince the executive not to enter the new market.

EXTRAPOLATION

When managers see a trend line fitted to a set of points on a graph, they frequently feel that they can make predictions about

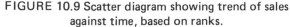

FIGURE 10.9 Scatter diagram showing trend of sales
against time, based on ranks.

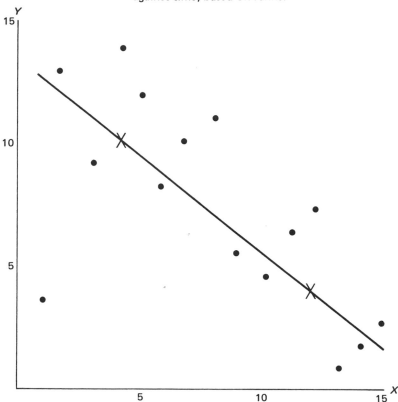

one of the factors simply by extrapolating or extending the line. Statisticians frown at the extrapolation of trend lines beyond the range of the observed data. They do so with good reason. Just because some factor has behaved in a certain manner in the past is no guarantee that it will continue to behave that way in the future. The further we attempt to extrapolate beyond the range of observed data, the more likely we are to make significant errors. And, of course, the greater the scatter of points about the line on the scatter diagram and the lower the absolute value of the correlation coefficient, the more risky extrapolation becomes.

Nevertheless, most intuitive decision makers do extrapolate. When decisions must be made about the future, the only information available is what has happened in the past. Consequently,

TABLE 10.8   Product sales, 1965 through 1979 (in millions of dollars).

Year X	Sales Y	Rank of X	Rank of Y
1965	152.1	1	4
1966	186.4	2	14
1967	171.0	3	10
1968	188.3	4	15
1969	185.2	5	13
1970	168.7	6	9
1971	177.4	7	11
1972	180.0	8	12
1973	155.8	9	6
1974	154.2	10	5
1975	160.7	11	7
1976	166.8	12	8
1977	143.2	13	1
1978	147.8	14	2
1979	150.1	15	3

TABLE 10.9   Computation of rank correlation coefficient for sales data over time.

Year X	Rank of X	Rank of Y	$X_r - Y_r$	$(X_r - Y_r)^2$
1965	1	4	$- 3$	9
1966	2	14	-12	144
1967	3	10	$- 7$	49
1968	4	15	-11	121
1969	5	13	$- 8$	64
1970	6	9	$- 3$	9
1971	7	11	$- 4$	16
1972	8	12	$- 4$	16
1973	9	6	3	9
1974	10	5	5	25
1975	11	7	4	16
1976	12	8	4	16
1977	13	1	12	144
1978	14	2	12	144
1979	15	3	12	144
				926

$$r = 1 - \frac{6\Sigma(X_r - Y_r)^2}{n(n^2 - 1)} = 1 - \frac{(6)(926)}{(15)(224)} = 1 - \frac{5,556}{3,360}$$

$$= 1 - 1.654 = -.654$$

decisions must be based on data about past occurrences. When extrapolation is necessary, it is better to use tools such as the ones discussed here than to rely on pure guesswork. As long as the decision maker is aware of the pitfalls, has applied the tools correctly, and doesn't try to extrapolate too far beyond the range of the data, these procedures can be of great help in decision making.

TESTING SOME BASIC ASSUMPTIONS

Every decision maker starts out with a set of basic assumptions about a decision situation. There are certain things that are given—certain facts that must be assumed. These assumptions provide the decision maker with some reference point from which to begin an analysis of the situation. Some basic assumptions need not and frequently cannot be tested. But others can and should be. The assumptions that should be tested generally relate to the source and validity of the observations on which the decision will be based.

Many types of decision problems require an assumption of homogeneity. More specifically, this means that observations obtained on different groups of individuals or from different sources really come from the same overall group or population. Consequently, the assumption to be tested is that there is *no difference* between two sets of observations, and the observations themselves will either verify or discredit the assumption.

There is a cliché that states that you can't compare apples and oranges. This simply means that when comparisons of some characteristic are to be made, the objects compared must be similar. For example, we might ask if the customers of downtown and suburban stores are alike in their shopping habits or are basically different. The answer to such a question would affect decisions regarding advertising, merchandise, store hours, and so on.

Some other assumptions of no difference that could be pertinent to business decision making include:

There is no difference in the managerial (or other) ability of males and females.

There is no difference in the mileage (or other) ability of different brands of gasoline.

There is no difference in the quality of output of machine tools manufactured by two different companies.

The piping in of recorded music has no effect on productivity.

There is no difference in the purchasing habits of residents of large cities and small towns.

Suppose that the president of a chain of retail stores is faced with problems related to merchandising, advertising, and promotion for all the stores. In the past, similar merchandise and the same advertising and promotional programs were used in all stores, regardless of whether they were located in downtown areas or in suburban shopping centers. This policy assumed that shoppers in both types of stores were similar in buying habits, preferences, responses to advertising appeals, and so on.

Suppose, however, that the president decides to test this assumption of no difference. To keep the example simple, assume that the first test compares the customers in terms of the size of their purchases. Other characteristics could be tested in the same way.

The president collects information by stationing an interviewer outside one downtown store and one suburban store. Each interviewer randomly selects ten shoppers as they leave the store and asks each one the amount of his or her purchase. This results in a set of ten numbers associated with shoppers at the downtown store and a set of ten numbers associated with the shoppers at the suburban store. We will let X represent the value of purchases made by the suburban shoppers and Y the value of purchases made by the downtown shoppers. Of course, in practice, samples would probably be obtained from more than ten shoppers in each group and from more than two stores.

Since there is bound to be some variability among the numbers in each set, it would be difficult for anyone to decide simply by looking at the numbers if the two sets were similar or if there was a significant difference between them. There is, however, a simple procedure for drawing such a conclusion. Each X value is paired with a Y value in a random manner. It is then necessary only to determine if X is greater than Y or less than Y. If X is greater than Y, a plus is marked next to that pair. If X is less than Y, a minus is marked. If, for any pair, X and Y happen to be equal, that pair is eliminated from the analysis.

The rationale for this procedure is as follows. If both sets of data are essentially alike—that is, if they come from one large, homogeneous population—then any X value is just as likely to be greater than a Y value as it is to be less than Y. Therefore, on the average, there should be about the same number of pluses and minuses. If there are too many pluses or too many minuses, we would have to reject the assumption of no difference. In order to determine what constitutes too many, we use the normal distribution and Z scores, as explained previously.

Suppose that the purchases of the downtown and suburban shoppers were as shown in Table 10.10. Notice that in the third column of the table the sign of the difference $X - Y$ appears for each pair of values. It is easy to determine that there are 6 minuses and 4 pluses. The question the decision maker must answer is whether this slight preponderance of one sign over the other is sufficient to conclude that the downtown and suburban shoppers really differ in the size of their purchases.

If we count the number of pluses and divide by the number of pairs, we obtain the proportion of pluses in the set of data. In

TABLE 10.10   Comparison of purchases between downtown and suburban shoppers.

Suburban Shoppers X	Downtown Shoppers Y	Sign of Difference $X - Y$
$14.98	$ 5.99	+
$ 6.59	$16.49	−
$19.49	$12.98	+
$ 3.98	$22.53	−
$ 5.98	$ 8.99	−
$ 9.49	$14.98	−
$12.69	$10.88	+
$ 3.59	$ 7.59	−
$31.36	$ 9.99	+
$12.38	$14.98	−

this case, the proportion is $4/10 = .4$. We will let p stand for the proportion of pluses and n represent the number of pairs of values. A Z score can be computed from the following equation:

$$Z = \frac{(p - .5)\sqrt{n}}{.5}$$

For this example, substitution of the actual values yields:

$$Z = \frac{(.4 - .5)\sqrt{10}}{.5} = \frac{(-.1)(3.2)}{.5} = -.64$$

A commonly used criterion for accepting or rejecting an initial assumption or hypothesis is to accept whenever the absolute value of the Z score is less than 2 and to reject whenever the absolute value is 2 or greater. (Absolute value means the value regardless of the sign, plus or minus, that precedes the number.) This criterion provides a risk of about 5% of incorrectly rejecting the assumption. Of course, other criteria involving smaller risks of error could be used, but in general a risk of 5% is considered acceptable. In this case, we could conclude that the slight preponderance of minuses over pluses is not sufficient to reject the assumption of no difference between downtown and suburban shoppers.

This test is quite simple to use, since it requires practically no arithmetic calculations. Observation is sufficient to determine whether one number is larger or smaller than another, and the only arithmetic required is the calculation of the Z score.

The test can also be applied when two observations are made on the same individual, as in the case of before-and-after observations. Suppose, for example, that several salesmen are sent to a sales training course. Their average weekly sales before the course might be compared with their average weekly sales after the course. The basic assumption in this case would be that there is no difference in sales—in other words, that the course has no effect on performance. A significant preponderance of one kind of sign over the other would, of course, suggest that the assumption should be rejected.

TESTING FOR OBJECTIVITY OR RANDOMNESS

In obtaining data for decision making, managers must for the most part depend on samples. In order for decisions based on sample data to be effective, the information from the samples must be valid and the samples must be representative of the population from which they are taken. Representativeness is assured by a random selection of sample members. However, true randomness is not always easy to achieve. Furthermore, many managerial decisions are based on data collected for other purposes, and the manager may have no control over the collection procedures. Samples that are not randomly selected might contain biases which may lead to erroneous conclusions.

Before basing a decision on information obtained from samples, the manager should conduct a simple test to verify their representativeness. The test requires that the sample values be classified into one of two mutually exclusive categories. Sometimes these categories will exist naturally in the population—for example, categories such as male and female, good and defective, foreign and domestic. When natural categories are not inherent in the data, they must be created. For numerical data, a convenient method is to classify values according to whether they are above or below some middle value, such as the median.

All observations are therefore classified as belonging to category A or category B. In performing this test, called the *runs test,* the original order of the observations must be maintained. The observations, represented by A's and B's, must be in their original order so that the number of runs can be counted.

A run is simply a sequence of identical observations preceded and followed by a different observation. For example, in the following sequence of A's and B's, there are 8 runs. Each run is underlined and separated from the others by a space: AAA B A BBBB AA BB AAA BB. Notice that a run can consist of a *single* observation if it is preceded and followed by a different observation.

The question that can be asked about such a sequence is: Do the A's and B's appear in a random order? This question is difficult to answer intuitively. In any random sequence, we would expect to see runs of varying lengths. However, too few runs or too many runs implies a lack of randomness. For example, the two following sequences appear not to be random for the reasons of too few and too many runs respectively:

$$\text{AAAAAAAAA BBBBBBBBB}$$
$$\underline{A}\ \underline{B}\ \underline{A}\ \underline{B}\ \underline{A}\ \underline{B}\ \underline{A}\ \underline{B}\ \underline{A}\ \underline{B}\ \underline{A}\ \underline{B}\ \underline{A}\ \underline{B}\ \underline{A}\ \underline{B}\ \underline{A}\ \underline{B}$$

The first sequence has only 2 runs in 18 observations, while the second sequence has 18 runs in 18 observations. The runs test provides a criterion for determining, for any sequence of observations, what constitutes too few runs and what constitutes too many.

For any sequence of observations of which n_1 are A's and n_2 are B's, we can test the assumption of randomness simply by counting the number of runs, which we will designate R, and determining on the basis of a Z score whether R is too small or too large for the sequence to be random. Computing the Z score is somewhat more complicated for this test than for the test of homogeneity, but the arithmetic is not difficult. The only additional requirement is that the sample contain a minimum of 20 of one kind of observation, either A's or B's.

The Z score is computed from the following equation:

$$Z = \frac{R - \dfrac{2n_1 n_2}{n_1 + n_2}}{\sqrt{\dfrac{2n_1 n_2(2n_1 n_2 - n_1 - n_2)}{(n_1 + n_2)^2 (n_1 + n_2)}}}$$

The same criteria for acceptance or rejection of the assumption of randomness can be used here as for the test of homogeneity in the previous section.

To illustrate, suppose that an interviewer for a consumer testing organization is stationed outside a store in a downtown shopping area to interview shoppers as they leave the store. In reviewing the completed forms submitted by the interviewer, a supervisor notes a certain sequence of male and female shoppers interviewed. The supervisor decides to test the sequence for randomness. Since the categories "Male" and "Female" appear naturally in the population, we will use a sequence of M's and F's instead of A's and B's:

$$\underline{FF}\ \underline{M}\ \underline{F}\ \underline{MMMM}\ \underline{FFFFF}\ \underline{M}\ \underline{FFF}\ \underline{MMMM}$$
$$\underline{F}\ \underline{M}\ \underline{FFFFFFF}\ \underline{M}\ \underline{F}\ \underline{MMMMMM}$$

Each run in the sequence is underlined. The total number of runs is 14. To determine if 14 runs in a sequence of this size is too few or too many for the assumption of randomness, we can compute the Z score using the following information:

Number of F's in the sequence $n_1 = 21$
Number of M's in the sequence $n_2 = 18$
Number of runs in the sequence $R = 14$

$$Z = \frac{R - \dfrac{2n_1n_2}{n_1 + n_2}}{\sqrt{\dfrac{2n_1n_2(2n_1n_2 - n_1 - n_2)}{(n_1 + n_2)^2(n_1 + n_2)}}}$$

$$= \frac{14 - \dfrac{(2)(21)(18)}{21 + 18}}{\sqrt{\dfrac{(2)(21)(18)[(2)(21)(18) - 21 - 18]}{(21 + 18)^2(21 + 18)}}}$$

$$= \frac{14 - \dfrac{756}{39}}{\sqrt{\dfrac{756(756 - 21 - 18)}{(39)^2(39)}}} = \frac{14 - 19.4}{\sqrt{\dfrac{(756)(717)}{(1,521)(391)}}}$$

$$= \frac{-5.4}{\sqrt{\dfrac{542,052}{59,319}}} = \frac{-5.4}{\sqrt{9.138}}$$

$$= -\frac{5.4}{3.0}$$

$$= -1.8$$

A Z score of 1.8, either positive or negative, is generally assumed to fall in the region of acceptance—in this case, acceptance of the assumption of randomness. Recall that our criterion is to accept a test assumption whenever the absolute value of the

Z score is less than 2. In deciding to reject an assumption for a Z score of 2 or greater, we assume a risk of approximately 5% of falsely rejecting the assumption of randomness. To reject with a Z score of 1.8 would increase that risk to slightly over 7%. Of course, it is the prerogative of the decision maker to assume any level of risk of error that he or she deems appropriate to the decision situation at hand.

SOME CONCLUDING THOUGHTS

This chapter has been devoted to a few decision-making tools that fall outside the formal intuitive decision-making model developed in earlier chapters. They are included here because they are a useful adjunct to the techniques described previously. These tools were selected because of their applicability to a wide variety of decision situations and because of their simplicity: they are both easy to apply and easy to understand.

Most of the calculations can be done in seconds with a pocket calculator or in minutes with pencil and paper. In many cases, reasonable approximations can be achieved without pencil, paper, or calculator. Recall that in the formal intuitive approach to decision making we are more concerned with ranges of values than with precise numbers. Therefore, reasonable approximations are frequently as valuable to the decision maker as exact calculations.

11

SOME FACTS
ABOUT COMMON FALLACIES

It has been said that a little knowledge can be a dangerous thing. This does not mean that knowledge, even a little bit, can be bad. It simply means that less than a thorough understanding of a subject can frequently lead to erroneous conclusions. It is unlikely that any area of human knowlege is filled with as many misunderstandings and fallacies as probability. To make matters worse, there is perhaps no other area in which so many believe that they know more than they actually do. This results, no doubt, from the popularity of lotteries and gambling in contemporary society.

Because probability is so important in quantifying the uncertainties in decision situations, it is essential that the decision maker divest himself of various widely held fallacies about probability and chance. Even a technique like the formal intuitive method cannot provide protection against poor decisions that result from misconceptions and personal bias. Since all information received or perceived by the decision maker must be interpreted, proper interpretation is necessary in order for the resulting probability assessments to be valid.

Decision making, even in large organizations, is often a very personal and subjective activity. It is impossible to eliminate all subjectivity from the decision-making process, even if it were desirable to do so. Although subjective evaluations are present in every phase of the formal intuitive method, they have their greatest impact in the assessment of the probabilities assigned to the uncertain states of nature. Preconceptions, misconceptions, and biases held by the decision maker can affect the validity of these assessments, which in turn could result in poor decisions.

Some of the decision criteria we have discussed—specifically, the criteria of optimism, pessimism, and neutrality—are dependent on the decision maker's general attitude toward the decision-making environment. As we have seen, consistent use of any one of these criteria would lead to unsatisfactory results in the long run. Therefore, we have adopted the expected value criterion in the formal intuitive method. This criterion gives the decision maker a great deal more latitude in expressing his uncertainties about the states of nature in terms of probabilities. However, in giving the decision maker greater latitude, it also provides him with more opportunity for error due to misconception and bias.

JUDGMENT AND BIAS

We have devoted considerable space and time to a discussion of the nature and validity of subjective information. Subjective assessments of state probabilities are bound to be affected by the attitudes and values of the decision maker. Differences in attitudes and values will most certainly affect any decision making process and must be accommodated in any decision-making technique if that technique is to result in optimal decisions. In the formal intuitive method, the assignment of probabilities to the states of nature is based on the judgment of the decision maker. Fortunately, as we have stated previously, most decision situations allow considerable latitude in the assignment of probabilities. In other words, the optimal decision is relatively insensitive to small and sometimes even moderate variations in the assigned probabilities. However, probabilities that are totally inconsistent with reality can lead to poor decisions and unfavorable consequences.

The subjective assessment of probabilities is based on the perceptions of the decision maker and his interpretation of what he perceives. The rationale for using subjective probability assessments is that intelligent and rational human beings, when presented with certain information, will produce probability assessments that are consistent with the information at their disposal. Furthermore, if several rational human beings are presented with exactly the same information, their probability assessments should be similar. If two people presented with the same information make radically different probability assessments, the difference is probably due to misconceptions or bias on the part of one or both of them.

A misconception and a bias are not the same thing. A misconception results from a lack of understanding about the phenomenon being observed. A bias is a preconceived notion that remains unchanged even in the face of contrary evidence. The concept of bias is exemplified by the statement "Don't bother me with facts; my mind is made up."

The so-called *gambler's fallacy* is an example of both misconception and bias. This fallacy applies to various games of chance in which the gambler can bet on one of two events that have roughly equal probabilities of occurring. Betting on the toss of a coin is one example. Betting on *red* versus *black* or *odd* versus *even* in roulette is another.

The fallacy is based on the assumption that every time a coin is tossed and a head fails to appear, the probability of getting a head on the next toss increases. As applied to roulette, the fallacy leads to the conclusion that every time a succession of odd numbers appears, each additional odd number increases the probability that an even number will appear on the next spin of the wheel. This is, of course, untrue. Neither a coin nor a roulette wheel has a memory. If the probability of getting a head on the first toss of the coin is .5, or 1/2, it is still 1/2 on the second toss, the tenth toss, and the hundredth toss, even if *all* the previous tosses resulted in tails.

The gambler's fallacy results from both misconception and bias. The misconception is a misunderstanding of the probability measure as it applies to a sequence of independent events. If the probability of getting a head on a single toss of a coin is 1/2, then the probability of getting three successive heads in three tosses of the coin is $1/2 \times 1/2 \times 1/2 = 1/8$. However, this probability of 1/8 applies to a *future* series of tosses. If we have already tossed the coin twice and observed two heads, the probability that the third toss will result in a head is still 1/2.

The bias that leads to acceptance of this fallacy results from wishful thinking. Many people want to believe that the probability of a head increases with each appearance of a tail, and no amount of explanation or demonstration will convince them otherwise. As a result, we inevitably find people standing near a roulette wheel in a gambling casino and counting the number of times a red or black or odd or even number appears consecutively before they place a bet on the color or number that hasn't appeared for several turns. And, despite the negative results, the fallacy persists in one form or another to the profit and delight of casino operators.

In order to be a successful decision maker, one must be free of both biases and misconceptions about the factors in the decision situation. This is true whether or not the formal intuitive decision-making method is used. Misconception can be eliminated by education. This simply means that the decision maker should learn as much as possible about all the factors involved in the situation before making a decision. Bias is much more difficult to eliminate. Bias can result from prejudice or simply from wishful thinking. In any decision situation the decision maker should examine his attitudes to determine if any biases are present. Once a bias has been identified, appropriate adjustments can be made. However, if decisions are made with existing biases, significant errors can result.

Many people subscribe to stereotypes about various groups or classes of human beings. Most of us realize that such stereotypes are misleading, and yet, consciously or unconsciously, we cling to them regardless of the facts. When this insistence on stereotypical images can lead to poor decisons with undesirable consequences, it is time to eliminate them from our thinking.

Frequently, probability assessments involve expressing the

likelihood that some individual comes from a particular class. In assessing such probabilities, we often rely on the criterion of *representativeness*. That is, if individual A has many of the characteristics we have attributed to group X, we assign a higher probability to his belonging to that group than we would had he lacked those characteristics. Representativeness is certainly a valid criterion to use in developing categories. The danger in this approach is that the characteristics attributed to the group might be completely unrealistic. Furthermore, if a decision maker holds strong biases either for or against some group, his probability assessments and consequently his decisions are more likely to be influenced by his biases than by any legitimate data available.

One of the major factors to be considered in assessing the probability of an event is its relative frequency of occurrence in some set of observations. Unfortunately, relative frequency is often ignored in favor of the criterion of representativeness, even when that criterion may be influenced by bias. Recently, an experiment was performed to determine whether most people rely more on relative frequency or on representativeness in assessing probabilities. Two sets of subjects were given personality profiles of several individuals supposedly selected at random from a group of lawyers and engineers. For each personality profile, the subject was asked to assess the probability that the person described was an engineer rather than a lawyer. One set of subjects was told that the group from which the profiles were selected consisted of 30 engineers and 70 lawyers. The other subjects were told that the group consisted of 70 engineers and 30 lawyers. Both sets of subjects produced almost identical probability assessments, despite the different information they received on the relative frequency of lawyers and engineers. Apparently, all the subjects based their assessments on their notions of which personality traits were typical of lawyers and which were typical of engineers—the criterion of representativeness—ignoring almost entirely the information about the relative frequency of each profession in the group.

It should be apparent that the relative frequency of lawyers or engineers in the group will have a significant effect on the probability that an individual selected at random from that group will be either a lawyer or an engineer. In this experiment, all the subjects were influenced so strongly by their bias—stereotypes of professions—that they ignored pertinent information that would have enabled them to assess the probabilities accurately. It is interesting to note that when the experiment was repeated with different subjects who were given the same information about relative frequencies but were not provided with the personality profiles, the relative frequency information was used correctly and the probabilities were assessed accurately.

Another source of bias is related to the availability of certain types of information. People often estimate the probability of some event by the ease with which they can recall the occurrence of similar events. For example, they may assess the probability of someone of a certain age having a heart attack by recalling the number of such occurrences among their friends and acquaintances. Similarly, people often assess the probability of success or failure of a particular business venture by recalling a list of business pitfalls that can easily be brought to mind.

The ease of recall or the availability of such information can be a useful device for assessing probabilities, since the more frequent events are usually recalled with greater ease than the less frequent ones. However, the availability of certain information is influenced by factors other than frequency, and total reliance on ease of recall or availability can often lead to incorrect assessments.

A similar experiment was conducted to determine the effect of bias due to availability on the assessment of relative frequency or probability. In this experiment, subjects were read a list of names of well-known personalities of both sexes and were later asked to judge whether the list they heard contained more men or women. Different lists were read to different sets of subjects. In some of the lists the men were more famous than the women. In other lists, the reverse was true. In every case, the subjects incorrectly judged that the sex with the more famous personalities was the more numerous. The results of this experiment suggest that when the probability of some class of event is based on the availability of data or the ease with which instances of that event can be recalled, a class whose occurrences are easily re-called will seem to be more numerous than an equal class of events whose occurrences are less easy to recall.

THE LAW OF AVERAGES

A great many decision makers invoke the so-called *law of averages* to justify their subjective assessment of probability. In the gambler's fallacy, discussed previously, the law of averages is often used to explain the erroneous assumption that if an even number occurs on five or six successive spins of a roulette wheel, chance will produce a corrective run of five or six odd numbers in order to even out the sequence.

To set the record straight, the law of averages is a myth. There is no such law or rule in mathematical science. There is, however, a law called the *law of large numbers*, which is often misinterpreted and is, no doubt, the source of the mythical law of averages. The law of large numbers simply states that in repeated trials of an experiment that can lead to the occurrence of an event with a probability of p, the relative frequency of the occurrence of that event will approach p as the number of trials of the experiment gets infinitely large.

To illustrate the meaning of the law of large numbers, as-sume that the event is the occurrence of a head on the toss of a coin. If the coin is fair, the probability of getting a head on a single toss is $p = .5$. Suppose that we toss the coin 100 times and observe 45 heads and 55 tails, a preponderance of 10 more tails than heads. The relative frequency of heads in that sequence of 100 tosses is 45/100, or .45. If we were to continue the experi-ment for another 900 tossess and observed an additional 450 heads and 450 tails, the total number of heads observed would be $450 + 45 = 495$ and the total number of tails would be $450 + 55 = 505$. We would still have 10 more tails than heads, but the relative frequency of heads would now be 495/1,000, or .495. In other words, without compensating for the prepon-derance of tails over heads in the first 100 tosses, the relative frequency of heads has gotten much closer to the true proba-bility of a head, which is .5.

Most people naturally expect to see one head and one tail in two tosses of a coin. However, no one would be particularly surprised if two heads occurred on the two tosses. In some longer sequence of coin tosses—say, ten—it is not unusual to see six heads and four tails or even seven heads and three tails. In fact, the latter event has a probability of about .117 which means that it will occur approximately 12% of the time. This is by no means a rare event.

The common misconception about chance and probability is that if seven heads occur in some sequence of ten tosses, chance will see to it that seven tails will occur in the next sequence of ten tosses in order to even things up. The law of averages is usually cited to justify that assumption. However, we have seen that the law of averages is a misconception or misinterpretation of the law of large numbers. As applied to this example, the law of large numbers simply states that the relative frequency of heads will approach .5 as the number of tosses in the sequence gets very large. It does not imply that in some relatively short sequence of tosses a preponderance of heads or tails will be corrected.

The previous misconception, that chance will correct runs of one type of occurrence by generating compensating runs of the other type, leads easily to a second misconception. If a run of one type of event—say, heads—inevitably leads to a correcting run of tails, then any sequence of heads decreases the probability of getting a head on the next coin toss and increases the probability that a tail will appear. In other words, the probability of a head or tail occurring changes every time the coin is tossed. This is patently untrue. There are certain types of events whose probabilities do change, but these events are related in such a way that the occurrence of one of them will affect the probability of occurrence of the others. Such events are said to be *dependent*. In analyzing the states of nature in a decision situation, the decision maker must always be on the lookout for such dependencies among states. For example, in the Thermocal case, discussed previously, are the state of the economy and the existence of competition dependent or independent? The decision maker should closely examine the assumption of independence in that case to be sure that it is justified.

If you have subscribed to the previous two misconceptions regarding independent events, you may easily fall into the following trap. If chance is a self-corrective process and if the probability of a head occurring increases after a sequence of tails, then you should be able to increase your probability of winning by waiting until you observe a sequence of one type of event before betting on the occurrence of the other.

As we have already noted, many people do this in playing roulette or other games in a gambling casino. What they fail to realize is that they are observing a continuing process. Every spin of the wheel is the beginning of a new sequence of occurrences. If they had not observed the results of the previous spins of the wheel, they would, no doubt, have little difficulty estimating that the probability of getting either an odd or even number on the next spin is approximately 1/2. However, if they have observed a sequence of odd numbers, they are likely to believe that the probability of an even number occurring on the next spin is higher than it was before. Yet what possible effect can their knowledge about the previous results have on the operation of the roulette wheel?

The gambler's fallacy we have been discussing is based on a situation involving two occurrences with equal probabilities. The fact that the probabilities are equal makes long sequences of one occurrence or the other unlikely, but not impossible. However, suppose that the probabilities of the two possible occurrences are not equal. The greater the inequality between these two probabilities, the more likely it is that we will see runs of the occurrence with the higher probability. Now consider a gambler who observes ten consecutive heads in ten coin tosses or ten odd numbers in a row on a roulette wheel. If he subscribes to the gambler's fallacy, he would now begin betting on tails or on an even number under the assumption that its probability of occurring has somehow increased. However, we know from the previous discussion that these probabilities do not change and that if the probabilities were equal at the beginning of the sequence, they are still equal. What, then, can we infer from a long sequence of heads or odd numbers?

First, we must reexamine the initial assumption that the two possible occurrences have approximately equal probabilities of happening. Can we be absolutely sure that this is true? It is possible that the coin we have been observing has two heads or that the roulette wheel has been fixed in some way. In other words, we could be observing a crooked game. A decision maker must always use the information at his disposal to make probability assessments. In addition, he must be prepared to revise these assessments if new information indicates that they were unrealistic. Consequently, having observed ten heads or ten odd numbers come up successively in a situation where heads–tails or odd–even was assumed to have equal probabilities, the decision maker should revise this initial assumption. Since the sequence of ten in a row is so unlikely under the assumption of equal probabilities, the wise decision maker will conclude that the occurrence of an odd number has a higher probability than the occurrence of an even number and that a head is a great deal more likely to appear on that coin than a tail.

Under these circumstances, the gambler would be wise to decide not to bet at all. However, if he must gamble—or, in the case of the decision maker, must make a decision—he should conclude that on the next toss of the coin or spin of the wheel, another head is more likely than a tail and an odd number is more likely to occur than an even number. These conclusions are, of course, the exact opposite of those that would result from applying the gambler's fallacy or the law of averages.

THE EXTRAPOLATION FALLACY

Another common fallacy is associated with extrapolation, a topic discussed briefly in the previous chapter. Extrapolation is based on the premise that the past can be used to predict the future. This is sometimes true, but more often it isn't. Economists and other business analysts are continually searching for trends and cycles in business and economic activity. When trends and/or cycles appear to be present in a series of observations, the process of extrapolation begins. The trend of past movements is extended into the future. A cyclical movement with its ups and downs can also be projected. Many analysts and managers believe that by projecting this past behavior into the future they can make an accurate prediction.

Decision makers must be wary about such projections. Sometimes they can be fairly accurate, at least in the short run. However, when the projections do result in accurate forecasts, it isn't simply because some line or curve on a graph has been extended. Predictions based on past performance will be valid only if the trends and cycles identified from past data are indeed real and not just coincidence. This means that a valid and concrete reason must exist for this behavior to follow the observed pattern and that the underlying causal factors for the behavior have been identified, analyzed, and explained. It also means that sound reasons exist for believing that these mechanisms will continue to govern the behavior of the factor that is to be forecast. Even when all these conditions are satisfied, extrapolation beyond the immediate future is very risky and is seldom, if ever, warranted. There are simply too many unknown factors that can change over time, causing such extrapolations to become extremely inaccurate. And basing decisions on inaccurate or erroneous information can have disastrous consequences.

12

SUMMING UP

There is no doubt that mastery of the techniques that comprise the formal intuitive decision-making method will take time, effort, and concentration. However, the situations that require managerial decisions can be very complex, and managers realize that there are no easy solutions to complex problems. But there are ways to simplify such problems and make them more amenable to solution. That is the crux of the formal intuitive method.

None of the procedures used in this decision-making method are inherently difficult. None requires any mathematics more advanced than simple arithmetic. What is required is logical thinking—and that, after all, is what managerial decision making is all about.

In Chapter 1, some claims were made about the improvement in decision-making performance that might be expected with the use of this method. No decision-making method under conditions of uncertainty can guarantee optimal decisions 100% of the time, but consistent use of the formal intuitive method should improve a decision maker's performance significantly. In contrast to the typical success rate of about 1 in 2 (50%), a success rate of

2 in 3 (67%) or even 3 in 4 (75%) is a reasonable expectation with this method. Furthermore, results should improve with practice. Each successive application of the technique will enhance the decision maker's ability.

The formal intuitive method is effective for several reasons. First, it forces the decision maker to study, understand, and describe his decision situation clearly, completely, concisely, and correctly. Second, it enables the decision maker to utilize all the information resources at his disposal, including his own knowledge, in a logical and consistent manner. Third, it requires the decision maker to deal with the uncertainty inherent in all managerial decision situations by quantifying it and using it in the decision-making process. Finally, it provides the decision maker with a reasonable, objective criterion for selecting a single and unequivocal alternative from the set of alternatives available.

In today's complex business and social environment, poor decision making is becoming too costly to be tolerated. Whether the decision maker is a corporate executive or a government official, the toss of a coin or its equivalent can no longer be considered an acceptable decision-making procedure. A much more scientific approach is necessary. This book has tried to provide such an approach without getting bogged down in complicated or difficult mathematical procedures. Nevertheless, as Arnold Kaufmann has pointed out,* the happy marriage of intuition and logic can be achieved through the use, where possible, of mathematical methods.

* Arnold Kaufmann, *The Science of Decision Making* (New York: McGraw-Hill, 1968).

APPENDIX

TABLE A.1 Factors for estimating the standard deviation from the average range.

Number of Observations in Subgroup n	Estimating Factor f	Number of Observations in Subgroup n	Estimating Factor f
2	1.128	21	3.778
3	1.693	22	3.819
4	2.059	23	3.858
5	2.326	24	3.895
6	2.534	25	3.931
7	2.704	30	4.086
8	2.857	35	4.213
9	2.970	40	4.322
10	3.078	45	4.415
11	3.173	50	4.498
12	3.258	55	4.572
13	3.336	60	4.639
14	3.407	65	4.699
15	3.472	70	4.755
16	3.532	75	4.806
17	3.588	80	4.854
18	3.640	85	4.898
19	3.689	90	4.939
20	3.735	95	4.978
		100	5.015

TABLE A.2   Table of areas for the standard
normal probability distribution.

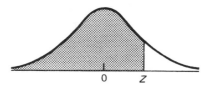

z	.00	.01	.02	.03	.04	.05	.06	.07	.08	.09
.0	.5000	.5040	.5080	.5120	.5160	.5199	.5239	.5279	.5319	.5359
.1	.5398	.5438	.5478	.5517	.5557	.5596	.5636	.5675	.5714	.5753
.2	.5793	.5832	.5871	.5910	.5948	.5987	.6026	.6064	.6103	.6141
.3	.6179	.6217	.6255	.6293	.6331	.6368	.6406	.6443	.6480	.6517
.4	.6554	.6591	.6628	.6664	.6700	.6736	.6772	.6808	.6844	.6879
.5	.6915	.6950	.6985	.7019	.7054	.7088	.7123	.7157	.7190	.7224
.6	.7257	.7291	.7324	.7357	.7389	.7422	.7454	.7486	.7517	.7549
.7	.7580	.7611	.7642	.7673	.7704	.7734	.7764	.7794	.7823	.7852
.8	.7881	.7910	.7939	.7967	.7995	.8023	.8051	.8078	.8106	.8133
.9	.8159	.8186	.8212	.8238	.8264	.8289	.8315	.8340	.8365	.8389
1.0	.8413	.8438	.8461	.8485	.8508	.8531	.8554	.8577	.8599	.8621
1.1	.8643	.8665	.8686	.8708	.8729	.8749	.8770	.8790	.8810	.8830
1.2	.8849	.8869	.8888	.8907	.8925	.8944	.8962	.8980	.8997	.9015
1.3	.9032	.9049	.9066	.9082	.9099	.9115	.9131	.9147	.9162	.9177
1.4	.9192	.9207	.9222	.9236	.9251	.9265	.9279	.9292	.9306	.9319
1.5	.9332	.9345	.9357	.9370	.9382	.9394	.9406	.9418	.9429	.9441
1.6	.9452	.9463	.9474	.9484	.9495	.9505	.9515	.9525	.9535	.9545
1.7	.9554	.9564	.9573	.9582	.9591	.9599	.9608	.9616	.9625	.9633
1.8	.9641	.9649	.9656	.9664	.9671	.9678	.9686	.9693	.9699	.9706
1.9	.9713	.9719	.9726	.9732	.9738	.9744	.9750	.9756	.9761	.9767
2.0	.9772	.9778	.9783	.9788	.9793	.9798	.9803	.9808	.9812	.9817
2.1	.9821	.9826	.9830	.9834	.9838	.9842	.9846	.9850	.9854	.9857
2.2	.9861	.9864	.9868	.9871	.9875	.9878	.9881	.9884	.9887	.9890
2.3	.9893	.9896	.9898	.9901	.9904	.9906	.9909	.9911	.9913	.9916
2.4	.9918	.9920	.9922	.9925	.9927	.9929	.9931	.9932	.9934	.9936
2.5	.9938	.9940	.9941	.9943	.9945	.9946	.9948	.9949	.9951	.9952
2.6	.9953	.9955	.9956	.9957	.9959	.9960	.9961	.9962	.9963	.9964
2.7	.9965	.9966	.9967	.9968	.9969	.9970	.9971	.9972	.9973	.9974
2.8	.9974	.9975	.9976	.9977	.9977	.9978	.9979	.9979	.9980	.9981
2.9	.9981	.9982	.9982	.9983	.9984	.9984	.9985	.9985	.9986	.9986
3.0	.9987	.9987	.9987	.9988	.9988	.9989	.9989	.9989	.9990	.9990
3.1	.9990	.9991	.9991	.9991	.9992	.9992	.9992	.9992	.9993	.9993
3.2	.9993	.9993	.9994	.9994	.9994	.9994	.9994	.9995	.9995	.9995
3.3	.9995	.9995	.9995	.9996	.9996	.9996	.9996	.9996	.9996	.9997
3.4	.9997	.9997	.9997	.9997	.9997	.9997	.9997	.9997	.9997	.9998

INDEX

233